# Change Management Adventures

# Change Management Adventures

**28 STORIES TO DEVELOP YOUR EXPERTISE**

## Jaap Boonstra

Warden Press

*For everyone who desires change*

ISBN:
Paperback: 978 94 92004 29 1
E-book (Epub): 978 94 92004 30 7
E-book (Mobi): 978 94 92004 31 4

© 2015 Jaap Boonstra

Original title: *Verandermanagement in 28 lessen* (Business Contact, Amsterdam, 2014)
Translated from the Dutch by Small Caps Bush Translations, Leiden
Cover design and lay-out: Sander Pinkse Boekproductie, Amsterdam
Cover illustration: Tony Feder © iStock
Portrait author: Wiep van Apeldoorn, Amersfoort
This edition published by Warden Press, Amsterdam

wardenpress.com
www.jaapboonstra.nl

Travelling is looking at yourself against a different background.

# Contents

## Imagining ambitions

## Travelling in the unknown

## Tackling the unexpected

## Looking for places to cross

## Resting and recuperating

## Reflections

# About this book

Change: many of us are right in the thick of it. Organisations are on the move in full swing, and that is certainly
something we notice, as managers, employees, advisors
and leaders. We are changing too, because we follow our
dreams and ambitions or because our dream is suddenly disrupted. People have even become professionals in
change. They work on change in positions such as change
manager, project leader, organisation advisor, entrepreneur and administrator. The lessons in this book are
reflections and inspiration for people involved in change.
There are various ways you can read this book.

*Are you a manager, entrepreneur or administrator?*
Take your time to look through the book. There is a good
chance you will pick up ideas you can use in the changes
you are involved in. The reflections in this book help you
give shape to change processes and invite you to reflect
on your own role. You will probably recognise yourself in
some of the stories.

*Are you a change manager, project leader or advisor?*
First take a look at what stage of the change you are working on, and start with the chapter which best suits that
stage. From there you can look ahead so you can avoid
pitfalls, or you can look back to use the stories as a learning experience. The lessons help you bring about those

changes successfully, and also help you develop further as a professional.

*Are you an employee in a company?*
Maybe an organisational change has just been announced, or you are in the middle of one; choose the lesson whose title stimulates or appeals to you the most. There is a good chance you will recognise things in the story. The lessons can help you not to wait and see, but to play a role yourself in the change.

*Are you a student who is interested in organisational change?*
In that case, it will be useful to read the book from cover to cover. The stories will give you a good impression of how a change process is built up and all the things it involves. If you want an overview first, you can also start with the reflections at the back. When you read some stories, you could be surprised at how simple change can be. Yet other stories will amaze you with the invisible complexities of change.

*Are you the partner of a manager or advisor?*
It is fun to read what all those people in organisations get so fussed about (and why your partner has to stay behind and work late so often!) There is certainly enough to laugh about in the stories in this book.

# Change is an adventure

Every year I go on a hike for a few weeks in the mountains to build up energy again. This trip gives me the space to contemplate and look back on the past year. I always ask myself three questions: What gave me pleasure and energy? Am I happy with what I am doing and who I am? What route do I envisage for myself for the coming year and the years after that? Hiking in the mountains is a real passion of mine: I love the beauty of nature and the peace it gives me while I am busy physically. For me, a mountain trip is an adventure I like to experience together with friends.

Changing organisations is also an adventure for me, just like a mountain trip through an unknown landscape. It is like an unorganised trip you tackle if you are well prepared yourself. It is rare to work on change alone, and that definitely does not happen in organisations. You look for your fellow travellers and companions and you set out together. According to a Chinese proverb, before you set out on a trip, you have to sit down. You wonder what the landscape looks like and what the climate is like. You choose your companions and ask them to travel with you. You check the map for differences in altitude and think about the possible routes. You discuss the nicest route with your companions and agree on what you will take with you.

You leave early on the first day: you want to enjoy the trip and you don't want to have to put your tent up too late. The map is useful for finding your way. But the map is not the landscape. The landscape is more colourful, more impressive, more changeable too. And what your map certainly doesn't show is the weather. The weather makes a big difference on a trip. A glorious day puts the whole landscape in a clear perspective and offers the most beautiful views. On a cloudy, rainy day you have no view any more, and you can't see the path properly. It can be rough, and you don't really want to relax in this weather. And yet, this kind of day with its hardships can also have its charm – although usually not till afterwards. If you are travelling through unknown territory, it is essential to keep a good eye on the weather conditions. If there is a snowstorm or thunderstorm, it can be wise to seek shelter and mark time. Of course you have a destination you want to reach, and you have planned your stages and rest days carefully. But it is not so much the destination which counts as the trip itself which provides enjoyment, which demands stamina, and in which you can enjoy the views.

If you prefer an organised trip with an agreed arrangement decided in advance, then this book is not right for you. But you do want to tackle the adventure? Well, come along on this trip with me. There are seven stages to our trip:

1. Orientation of the area;
2. Getting to the bottom of the area;
3. Imagining ambitions;
4. Travelling in the unknown;
5. Tackling the unexpected;
6. Looking for places to cross;
7. Resting and recuperating.

Would you like to come along?

# Orientation
# of the land

When we set out on a journey, we start by familiarising ourselves with the area. We gather information and try to form a picture for ourselves. We look where the nicest views are and the most difficult parts. We examine the options with an open mind. What is our idea, what do we have in mind? What kind of landscape or area do we want to explore, and what kind of adventure do we want to take on? We exchange pictures and experiences and choose where our journey will start.

# 1
# Strategically naïve

*The quality of untamed curiosity*

At university I learned you should make a competition analysis before you map out a route for organisational change. So it was only logical for me in my first change assignment to ask the board chairman, Richard, whether I could have the annual reports of the most important rivals for the past five years. Richard hesitated briefly before answering.

'Ah... yes, of course. I'll make sure you have them within two weeks.'

And indeed, within two weeks I had a pile of annual reports of the competition on my desk. It was very exciting to analyse those reports. Richard was also extremely interested in the analyses I made, and we had absorbing discussions about them. It was my own personal fascination to go deeply into the effects of new information systems on people's work and the organisation of the work processes. I found it curious that so few people had a picture of the work processes. All of them had various diagrams with organisation charts, but I didn't find these all that interesting. It was more fascinating to find out how a question or wish of a customer went through all kinds of departments and what those departments did with them. I had wonderful conversations with everyone I asked about what they did precisely. It did amaze me that the work had to go through so many channels, and that it took such a long time before a customer got answers to their question. Richard's attention was riveted each time I shared my observations with him.

I was surprised when Richard asked whether I would like to join the team which was supervising a merger. Without really thinking about the question, I replied immediately: 'Yes, that would be nice.'

Four weeks later, Richard asked me how things were going in the merger team.

'Well, you can forget the word "team", because that is one thing it certainly is not,' I answered impulsively.

'What do you mean, not a team?' he asked me.

'Nobody is working together. There is a *leaden-footed* member in the team who doesn't want to change anything at all, a *scaredy-cat* who won't take any risks, and a *watchdog* who just protects his own interests.'

After listening to my answer, Richard gave me a penetrating look. A smile appeared on his face: 'Wouldn't *you* like to be project leader of the merger team?'

'Yes, sure,' I answered, 'but then it has to be a different team.'

And that is how I became project leader of a merger process. At the time I thought it was quite normal, even though I had only just turned twenty-six.

The merger was completed successfully, and of course I was proud of the result achieved. At the end, I looked back over the period with Richard. I asked him why he had hesitated when reacting to my request for the annual reports of rival companies, and why he had asked me to be project leader. His answers taught me a great deal.

'We didn't have any reports at all of our rivals. Your question made me realise that in our company we didn't understand our market and our rivals enough, and that the strategy department was not working on competitive strategy in any case. Your question was very helpful for me and for the company. I asked you to be project leader because your youthful enthusiasm and frankness are stimulating for others. What's more, you were the only person in the company who was not worried about jobs and what the tools should look like, and the only person who really understood the work processes and the best way to organise them. And you asked the right questions every time: the questions we never ask ourselves because it is all so self-evident. But in mergers nothing is self-evident, that's when you have to reinvent everything. I thought the best moment was when you came to me, dejected, because of a conflict you had with one of the directors. When you explained to me so openly what had gone wrong, I realised that it very rarely happens that someone comes to me to tell me about something he hasn't done right. Since that time I have been much more conscious in my dealings with weak signals, and I have delved more deeply into discussions. You taught me a great deal with your untamed curiosity and your open questions.'

I have retained my curiosity and I still ask frank questions. Mapping out work processes continues to fascinate me, as does talking with people who do the work. Knowledge of customer processes and work processes is essential if you want to achieve change. It doesn't hurt to know your rivals and what is going on in the wider surroundings. Untamed curiosity is necessary where change is concerned.

It was only later that I realised that the merger's success was not due to me, but that I had been coached almost invisibly by someone who gave me confidence and enjoyed seeing others grow in their role. Richard gave me the space and confidence and was always available if I sometimes didn't know any more what I was doing. I learned a lot from him.

## 2

# Despondent

*Taking your feelings seriously and getting involved*

20  At a certain moment, I received a call from a bank director. Whether he could invite me for a discussion about a change process happening at the bank. He wanted to hear my opinion. He already hinted during the telephone call that the change was not going entirely according to plan. That aroused my curiosity, and I decided to accept his invitation.

I reported to the bank reception on a Tuesday afternoon. It was a stately hall with classical paintings of beautiful landscapes and portraits of dignified people. Someone came for me quickly, and I was taken to a room where an older gentleman came towards me.

'Good of you to come. I would like to hear your view on a change process we are working on here.' And he got straight down to business. 'We are working on the integration of bank and insurance activities. We are convinced that this is the future. It is how we can serve our customers better and offer them more products. We started off well and explained everything clearly. But once we started on the implementation, it turned out that not a lot was actually clear. We didn't get a step further.'

I asked professionally: 'What exactly did you do?'

His answer showed that the new business concept had been presented firmly. A project group had been appointed with managers from both sections, and they had been given clear instructions.

'How did it go then?' I asked calmly.

This question was followed by a deep sigh. 'We did all kinds of things. The business processes were identified and listed, we set up a front office and a back office, sales managers were appointed and trained, we developed new services and put them on the market.' As the director said this, I started feeling worried. 'What did these actions result in?'

There was a moment of anxious silence. 'In a big mess. We have not made any progress at all. The people from the bank business didn't want anything to do with insurance. And the insurers had all kinds of reasons why they believed banks and insurances could not go together. The director of bank affairs and the director of insurance no longer speak to each other, the integration is stuck and the project leader is at home with a serious nervous breakdown.'

My worried feeling grew and while I thought about how awkwardly they had tackled this, I asked: 'Has the customer noticed anything?'

The director looked gloomy. 'Nothing... well, nothing positive. The wealthy customers especially have complaints. They say they have to deal with too many people and they are offered products they don't want. Actually they are very clear: they want convenience, but they get fuss.'

I began to feel increasingly despondent, but still asked another question. 'What have you done yourself about this so far?'

Another silence, which now became painful. 'Hmm, I managed the strategy process together with the external agency. I appointed the project leader and gave him a clear assignment, and of course I told the directors that they really had to cooperate with each other.'

While he spoke, I could only think: this is terrible. This man earns six hundred thousand a year and has done everything clumsily. He has no vision and does not assume leadership. I felt despondent and everything in me screamed that I should not want to be involved in this change in any way. At the same time, I felt a knot in my stomach and I realised that I could not behave professionally if I felt that way about him. What do you do in that kind of situation?

I reacted from my feelings. 'Your story makes me feel very despondent. I don't see any role for myself in this.'

The director gave me a surprised look. 'Do you feel that way too? I thought I was the only one.'

His look changed and his posture now revealed dismay. So there we sat.

He continued quietly: 'What makes you feel despondent?'

I told him I had the impression that everything had been tackled extremely stupidly, that I had been working for years to share knowledge about change and that I had apparently not succeeded in that.

The director was visibly shocked. After a moment, he asked with an emotional voice: 'But don't you want to share your knowledge precisely in this situation?'

Once there is some rapprochement on an emotional level and you have looked each other deep in the eyes, you have laid the basis of the relationship, and it is difficult to break that. Only when everyone dares to reveal their weak side in a discussion does it become worthwhile to get down to work together. I took on the change process at this bank together with the director, and we learned a lot from the process and from each other. The most important learning experience is perhaps that new energy can arise from despondency and appreciation can grow from rapprochement. It is precisely at the start of a change process that relationships of trust are essential so that you can make something of it.

# 3

# Know what you stand for

*Open-minded observation and*
*appreciative inquiry*

After fifteen years of consultancy work in the financial

sector, I wanted to direct my efforts towards education, youth care and safety in neighbourhoods and districts. At the time there was a shortage of teachers and high rates of student dropouts and violence in education. My attention was drawn by a series of newspaper articles about a private school in a rural area.

'A capitalistic profiteer who must be stopped' was one headline. 'This is a typical example of a divide in society where rich people can organise good education for their children and other children remain disadvantaged,' was the line of another newspaper article. 'As far as special education is concerned, there has to be space for it and otherwise it should be forbidden,' was a third opinion.

Clearly something was going on here, since the newspapers were full of it. Because education fascinated me, I decided to contact the principal of that private school.

'Good afternoon. This is Jaap Boonstra. I have worked for some time on issues in education. You and your school are currently in all the newspapers. I wondered whether I might be able to come and talk with you.'

The voice on the other end of the line was friendly. 'Of course! You are very welcome. When would you like to come?'

I was a little surprised by this reaction. 'But aren't you very busy? You are in all the newspapers.'

The answer was striking: 'Oh Mr Boonstra, I may be in all the newspapers and they may talk a lot about me, but nobody talks with me. You are the first person to call. You are very welcome.'

One Wednesday afternoon I went to the school. The school gave a familiar impression. I was greeted by David, the principal. In his office, I opened the conversation to break the ice: 'May I ask you something: why did you start a private school?'

David looked at me: 'That's a long story. You should know that education is my life's passion. It energises me to see the future in the eyes of children. I am a teacher, and that is what I stand for. I used to be a principal at a small school in the province of Friesland. That was fantastic. You knew all the children and all the parents. The school was part of the community. But at a certain moment the school became too small to qualify for funding. We merged with another school, and I was principal of the merged school. That process repeated itself six times. I ended up being principal of a combined school with 900 students. All I was doing was rosters, regulations, building maintenance, funding, educational innovation, you name it. But I never saw students any more. I lost my passion, and I had a serious breakdown. That gave me the chance to reflect on what I actually stand for. I am a teacher and I want to contribute to the future of children. That is my profession, and that is what I want to do. My dream was to work again in a small school where I would know all the parents. Because if you know the parents, you know the students. You know what is happening and you can experience the children in person in their development. The school becomes part of the community again. I calculated that I can know about 150 parents personally. That works out at a school of around 100 students. But that didn't work, because it wasn't in line with the guidelines.

I tried everything: discussions at the ministry, compensation arrangements, experiment requests. Nothing was possible. The only thing I could do was start my own private school.'

I was impressed by his story. I asked David: 'But what about the shortage of teachers?'

'Well, I don't have that problem at all. The news that here we really pay attention to the students again is spreading like wildfire. I get twelve open applications every week from people who want to come and work here.'

'And sickness absence? How do you cope with that? That was another argument for large-scale education.'

That was not a problem according to David. 'Absence is due mainly to pregnancy. Well, you know that months in advance, so you can arrange things. And for long-term sickness absence you can also find solutions fairly fast. It is absolutely no problem to take care of short-term absence: those are the best lessons of all.'

I looked at him in astonishment. 'Yes, that's when we ask parents to jump in. We know them all. They come and give lessons about their profession or their passion. You couldn't wish for better career information. Often they are the most inspiring lessons. And the parents feel even more involved with the school that way too.'

'And violence at school?'

Now David looked at me in astonishment: 'We know all the students and their parents. We know what kinds of issues are at hand. Violence doesn't happen here. If it were to happen, we would see it coming and work on it.'

The idea that this was a capitalist profiteer could be thrown out. There was no question of a divide in education. Special education or not, that was beside the point. David knows who he is and what he wants to be. He took the initiative on his own and made renewal possible. If you know what you stand for, you are prepared to go against the flow and bring about renewal.

David's story ended up at the Education Council. The Education Council advised the minister to make space for small-scale education again, and this kind of education is now possible again. Renewal does not take place in the heart of the system but on the periphery, where people are able to make the difference. The question is whether you are prepared to postpone your judgement and start looking with an open mind, and whether you are capable of enquiring appreciatively about what is going on.

# 4
# Scarcity and abundance

*Looking for power for renewal*

The mood in Europe is gloomy. We live in one of the wealthiest and safest continents in the world, and yet we complain about a lack of safety and quality of life. Our children are among the happiest in the world, but we believe that teachers and youth workers don't do their work properly. We grumble about rising healthcare costs, the raised pension age, the level of unemployment and trains that are not punctual. We seem to lack everything, and we pay more attention to the scarcity than to the wealth in our lives.

Just when the discussion about scarcity and the need for new cuts flared up in Europe, I was in South Africa in Soweto, a township of Johannesburg. Approximately four million people live in Soweto in around 90 neighbourhoods. Unemployment is at 60% and poverty is rife. Most people live in slum dwellings made from corrugated iron and cardboard. AIDS is a big problem. For many people, Soweto evokes images of violence, rape, murder, riot and danger. And it was like that, ten years ago. Soweto was a 'no-go area' abandoned by the official authorities of Johannesburg. The police would not go there. There was scarcely any schooling. Rubbish was not collected and it piled up. The situation seemed hopeless. Until artist Mandla Mentoor took the decision that he did not want to live in a neighbourhood where art was not possible.

'I was facing a choice: who and what did I want to be? I want to be Mandla, a proud, black artist who contributes to life through his art. But what could I do in an environment where there is nothing? And yet I knew that if I did nothing myself, there was a good chance I would become a murderer or be murdered, instead of being an artist.'

The starting point for renewal was getting children together whose parents had died of AIDS. The children planted flowers on the edge of a hill which had changed into a towering rubbish dump. Mandla related: 'Every situation has possibilities and hope for improvement. Every situation also has energy and positive force for renewal. The trick is to discover them. You have to understand that Soweto is a black township. The black community respects nature, ancestors and children. From that positive force it was easy to get children together to plant flowers for their deceased parents.'

When Mandla asked the children whether they wanted to continue to live in this dead-end situation, their answer was: 'No!' But what could they do? There was a lack of work, schooling, healthcare, safety. But then they turned their thinking around and gave the hopeless situation new meaning: there was an abundance of manpower, of raw materials in the form of waste, and of energy to want to make the difference.

Under Mandla's guidance, children started to regard waste as a raw material. Waste was collected and sorted. Plastic was used to make hats and bathmats. Old paper was turned into new paper which schools could use. Unusable paper was used for papier-mâché which served as a material for art. Old barrels were turned into musical drums. This stimulated other people to make other musical instruments from the mountain of waste. Art and music thus came into existence, the mountain of waste was eliminated and people in the neighbourhood found a new identity. When I asked what was so nice about making music,

Phaswane, a black drummer of about sixteen, answered: 'It's nicer to make music than to kill people. Where I grew up, there was a lot of murder happening. I faced the choice of having to commit murder or being murdered myself. I have left those times behind. Making music is much nicer.' The same Phaswane now travels the world with his music group and a youth dance group, making music and dancing. The money he earns through this goes back to the community.

Now, more than twenty groups are active in the neigh-bourhood. Besides the music group and the art group there are also groups for waste processing, environmental design, education, clothes repair, meals, dance, media and tourism. The groups organise themselves. They meet regularly to ask each other questions, give advice, support each other and develop new initiatives. There is no rubbish in the neighbourhood any more. The rubbish dump has gone back to being a hill with a park-like landscape where people from adjacent neighbourhoods can meet each other. The old water tower on the hill, previously a hiding place for youth gangs, is now a symbol of renewal. The discarded car tyres, previously used for necklacing murders, now serve as building material for a community house. Murder, rape and robbery have become rare. From the basis of identity, giving meaning and self-organisation, a new community has arisen which shapes its own future. The transformation goes even further. The music and dance groups are by now causing an international furore. Their success has made them an example and a support for new groups of young children who are learning to make music and who can dance again. A new group has been formed whose members want to tell their story about the quality of life in their neighbourhood to people in other neighbourhoods in Soweto. Duduzile, a fifteen-year old girl, says: 'We are going to tell people our story, we are going to show our enthusiasm. We are going to invite them to come and have a look at our place. We will ask them whether they want to share their experiences, because we can only make a difference if we do that together.'

If you know who you are and who you want to be, you can take unusual initiatives. Mandla Mentoor taught me that even in the most hopeless of situations there is space for renewal by looking at what *is* there, where there is positive energy and asking yourself who would like to participate. By having a look at unusual places as a leader, professional or advisor, you learn to look at your own environment differently, and you start to see new possibilities. Of course that raises questions: do you dare set foot in a place which is strange and dangerous? It is precisely in that place that you can pick up new ideas. Roaming through an unknown area helps you look at yourself and your environment differently. When you examine existing situations with an appreciative look, you see the power which is present and the beauty. Instead of scarcity you see an abundance of possibilities.

   Entering a different culture with an open view helps you to look differently. Francis Picabia's statement is all too true: *'Our heads are round, so our thoughts can change direction.'* That can come in handy when we are exploring the surroundings and want to understand what is going on.

# Getting the lay of the land

Once we have an initial idea about where we want to go, we study the landscape, the people who live there and the climate in more depth. We want to get the best possible idea of what we can expect, and sort out possible routes. We want to know what and who we might encounter in the area. We also choose our travelling companions. We actually already build an impression of the area and the challenges it holds for us.

# 5

# Coming clean

*Cultural differences as a source of change*

I went to Finland a few years ago. A company there had
invited me for a discussion about product innovation.
Management was struggling with the issue of the best way
to organise the development of new products. There were
two opposing opinions. The marketing people wanted
to put the development function with the business units,
because they had the information about customer wishes.
But the technical staff saw more in a central development
function which could make optimum use of new technical
possibilities. Top management had not made any decision yet, but had invited me to come and think along with
them.

I reported to the company on a Tuesday afternoon. 'Ah,
yes, it's you. Welcome – we were expecting you. You're
a bit early, but that's not a problem. You can already go
through to the meeting venue. It's downstairs. Take those
stairs there.'
   I took the stairs and unexpectedly ended up in a sauna
complex. There was no-one to be seen. Just when I
started wondering whether I was at the right place, a man
came down the stairs. 'Hello, welcome! You must be Mr
Boonstra. It is so good that you are here.' The man introduced himself and then started to take his clothes off. I
was standing there watching rather uncomfortably when
Aarne, the board chairman, also came downstairs. He

welcomed me warmly and asked how my trip had been. Then he started undressing too. When he saw my rather astonished look, he burst out laughing. 'Oh, of course, I didn't tell you that when I met you last. We always hold our strategic discussions downstairs here, and first we enjoy a sauna together.'

Fifteen minutes later I was sitting with eleven naked men and women in a very hot sauna. For a quarter of an hour not a word was said in the sauna: we all just sweated. Then everyone took a cold shower, jumped in an ice-cold immersion bath, put on a bathrobe and went to the relaxation area. There Aarne gave a brief explanation of the central themes and clarified what was at stake for the company. He invited his colleagues to reflect on their own point of view and put themselves in other people's shoes. This was followed by twenty minutes of relaxation and silence. At the end of this sauna session a glass partition was opened and we entered a light room with a table laid out with fruit and fruit juices. Aarne took the floor again to explain the key question, and he invited the people present to share their perspectives. The viewpoints were calmly put forth. Then everyone looked at me, and I was asked if I would like to share my experiences in the organisation of production innovation. The presentation I had prepared did not suit this setting and was superfluous anyway. I had taken the time in the sauna to think evenly about the subject matter. While relaxing, I had looked more closely at the meaning of that subject matter for the company and the existing points of view. The atmosphere was peaceful and open, and I was able to contribute my experiences and answer questions in an even and composed way. After forty-five minutes of discussion, no further views emerged. Aarne thanked everyone for their contribution, summarised the points of view and made the decision about how the compa-

ny would organise the innovation of products. It was a
well-considered decision.

Afterwards I walked together with Aarne. He apologised
in his office that he hadn't told me how strategic discussions always started with a communal visit to the sauna.
It was so natural for him and his colleagues. In turn, I told
him that I was very impressed. A difficult and important
decision had been made within one-and-a-half hours –
something people in other European companies might
squabble about for months.

'A sauna helps. Everyone is exposed, feels the heat,
understands the importance. And you get a communal
atmosphere. What's more, people leave their operational
concerns behind and space is created so they can think
strategically.'

I recognised what Aarne was telling me, and while he
looked at me with a smile on his face, he asked: 'But I think
you visit the sauna quite often and you also dare to bare all,
or am I wrong?'

It does not hurt to take a break when difficult decisions
are involved. You can use that peace and quiet to allow the
essence of the decision to get through to you. Nor does
it hurt to put yourself in the shoes of the other person. It
helps in change processes to seek out the heat and make
it possible to discuss differences. New points of view from
unknown players can help loosen up fixed viewpoints. All
this creates space for examining your own situation in a
different way, and looking for solutions which go further
than the earlier conflict.

Different cultures and different points of view are often
a source of amazement and confusion. Sometimes those
differences can result in awkwardness or conflict, but
cultural confrontations almost always lead to new insights
about yourself, your company, and the other party. This
helps create space for strategic renewal. At the start of

change processes, the trick is to examine the issue at hand in a different way, to look at the players opposing each other and possible solutions which go beyond the beaten track.

# 6
# Scaredy-cats

*About entering the discomfort zone*

There is a lot happening in youth care. Professionals do their utmost to contribute to the future of children, but that is not always simple. Take a standard multi-problem family. Father drinks and beats mother. Mother requires psychiatric treatment because of this. Junior has been taken into care because of the unsafe situation at home. The other son, fourteen years old, can look after himself. He is finished with school (he believes) and is very pleased with his new scooter (nobody knows how he came by it). The daughter has been placed in a safe environment because she is under the influence of a pimp boyfriend. This family receives support from twelve care providers from youth care, social assistance, neighbourhood help, debt assistance, mental healthcare, social work, education, the police, and the housing corporation. The policies of seven ministries affect the family, which results in significant policy pressure. This weighs heavily on youth care professionals and that does not help the family.

I once invited fifteen government officials to experience the implementation of the youth policy by visiting a problem neighbourhood with me one afternoon and talking with problem families. This led to a heated discussion. 'Look here, you can't just go and do that,' was the first reaction to my invitation. That made me curious, and I delved deeper. There were numerous arguments. Some arguments were about the person's own understanding of their role: 'It doesn't fit in with my duties,' 'There are other people for that,' 'I already know how things are there,' 'That is not in my job description,' 'I have not been instructed to do that,' 'But that's not strategic,' 'I really won't get the space to do that,' 'I don't have the budget for that' and 'I have no time for that because we have to keep going'. There were also arguments which revealed a certain powerlessness: 'Yes, but if I raise expectations which I can't fulfil…' or 'Yes, but if I have to do something with that and

it doesn't fit within the policy…' Other objections pointed more to fear: 'There's no sense in doing that, those people don't trust the government anyway,' 'Yes, but what if you come across journalists there?' and 'Who guarantees that it's not dangerous for us to visit that neighbourhood?' It was a pity, because I had already organised a bus so we could travel together and share our experiences.

Apparently it was not self-evident to go and have a look at where policy was meant to have an effect. To my mind, open-minded observation in the zone of discomfort is the basis for taking strategic action. How you can develop policy if you don't know what is going on?

The discussion continued. So how would you visit the zone of discomfort as a public servant without being trapped or threatened? This turned out to be a bit more difficult to think up, but gradually several ideas emerged: 'If we don't go as a group, but just go and sit on a bench on the square on our own or in pairs, you see a lot and you're bound to strike up a conversation with someone. You could also go to the schoolyard at the end of the school day and start talking with the parents coming to pick up their children. I would like to make it a photo project; I could ask people to take photos of me too. And at the market you can just ask people what they think makes the neighbourhood attractive. We could buy some chips in that snack bar which has been held up five times, and eat them there. Or we could go to a Moroccan tea house or a Turkish restaurant to have a meal. We could also talk with police officers and with people from the housing corporations. Isn't there a soccer pitch there too?'

In the end it turned out to be simple to do some exploration, meet people and get discussions going about the issues in the neighbourhood. And it didn't stop with just one visit. The exchange of experiences was stimulating, and it helped all the people involved to think differently about their own policy area. 'At a certain moment we were simply with the people in their own homes. We would be invited in for a cup of tea and we had fantastic conversations. When they asked what we did, we told them we were civil servants and that we wanted to experience what the problems were for ourselves. They said: 'Then you are good civil servants who are at least really interested in normal people.'

If you do not go out and explore, you cannot observe with an open mind and you will not enter into a discussion; viewpoints will stay the same and new ideas just won't get a chance. Open-minded observation and entering into discussion are highly strategic if you are looking for solutions to social problems. That is why a good strategist is never busy.

It is really quite simple to act strategically if you dare to enter the zone of discomfort with an open mind. You don't have to do that as a civil servant or government official. You can also just show your interest and enter into a conversation as a human being.

# 7

# Sex

*Breaking through taboos to get to the core*

The large merger process in which I played a part was tense. And not just for me. Managers and employees were uncertain about what was going to happen. All kinds of things would change, that was for sure. The ambition was to break through the compartmentalisation of departments so that customer service could improve. An analysis of the business processes showed that it would be better to amalgamate the departments concerned with business operations. That analysis had been carried out with great care, I thought.

'No, that is really very unwise, amalgamating those depart- ments,' one of the department heads told me. 'You're bringing processes together which would be better staying separate, from the viewpoint of control and separation of functions. The accountants will never agree to it.' This was a viewpoint I had not considered, so I went back to work on the analysis of the business processes and consulted the accountants.

'That amalgamation is no problem at all,' was the accountant's answer to my question. 'Actually, it is a good idea. It will be better for efficiency and will provide admin- istration with much better support. I would go through with it.'

Back I went to the department head who had expressed his objections earlier. 'But it is a bad plan. You are bringing processes together which require totally different systems, and you are also mixing short-term activities and long-term activities. Those long-term activities will suffer from the pressure of the short-term activities. You don't think we organised those departments separately for nothing, do you?' The department head put his arguments forward forcefully. And again I went back to do my homework all over.

My detailed analysis gave no support for the arguments of the department head. What's more, the acquisition of a new integrated system would make simplification possible. This would improve services and the costs would end up significantly lower. I felt uncomfortable with my analyses. Every time I looked, the benefits of the amalgamation became more and more evident. But the counter arguments were also expressed increasingly forcefully. I decided to go back to the department head. I chose a calm moment at the end of the afternoon for the conversation.

'No, really, it simply won't work, that amalgamation is the stupidest thing you can do.' The department head was clearly still dead set against the merger.

'Why is it unwise?' I asked calmly.

'Well, it's just not on, it is a bad idea, you are endangering the whole of the business operation.' Real arguments were not provided. But the tone became increasingly emotional.

'I don't understand. I have carried out my analysis three times now, and each time it seems only more sensible to combine the departments. Tell me what makes it so difficult for you.'

There was a moment of silence. The department head looked at me. He was upset. 'Look, it's difficult to tell... Ah, I can't talk about it... It has to stay secret.'

'I promise it will stay between us, you can trust me on that,' I answered.

After some hesitation, the truth came out: 'You must

know I am married. Very happily married, and we have two great children. But I have a sexual relationship with someone in the other department. Nobody knows anything about it. I don't know what I would do if those departments were combined and I became her boss. It just wouldn't work.'

The departments were eventually integrated and the department head became the head of the new department. The lover found a good position in a different department.

The new department functions better than before. The department head later apologised to me and thanked me for taking him seriously each time and setting to work without taking it higher up. He was pleased that he had taken me into his confidence, because the integration of the departments was good for the business operation but he had really had no idea how to handle the situation and that had troubled him deeply.

This occurrence has enriched my view of organisations. Not everything is rational in organisations. Appearances are deceptive. Things that seem rational aren't always so, and arguments sometimes conceal the issues that are really at hand. There is invariably a story behind irrational arguments. The question is whether you can get that story out in the open by taking the teller and his story seriously. Some topics are difficult to talk about. Like sex. Through this experience I discovered that sex at work is far more prevalent than I had ever dreamed.

# 8
# Convincing and communicating

*Making real contact in an open dialogue*

The diagnosis was highly successful, and in the project team we had gained a good understanding of the problems of the organisation. The environmental scan had provided a clear perspective of chances and threats for the organisation. The competition analysis gave a good picture of the strengths and weaknesses of the company. The business processes were identified and listed, with the most striking aspect being the huge complexity. But we were most enthusiastic about our questionnaire survey. All the employees and managers were given a questionnaire. This was done in separate groups, as we were afraid that employees would not want to complete the lists if managers were present. Everything had to remain confidential. The questionnaire had given us a clear picture of the workflows, the problems occurring in the work, work motivation, the appreciation of the management style, the company culture and the employees' attitude towards the work and the managers. There was a huge response: more than 80 percent, and even higher for managers. A wonderful result. We knew how things worked there, and that gave us a picture of what had to change.

The feedback of the results from the diagnosis to the groups of employees went extremely well. The outcomes were shared in clear presentations. Three questions were distributed with post-it notes beforehand: What do you recognise? What surprises you? What do you have a question about? The post-its with the comments were stuck on a wall. That formed the basis for a discussion about the outcomes, which arose almost automatically. There was mainly a lot of recognition, certainly as far as the unclear strategy and the role of the managers was concerned. The complexity of the customer and business processes surprised nobody. What was surprising was that the far-reaching task specialisation resulted in enormous waiting times and that customers were dissatisfied with that. You could feel the energy in the group meetings, and the will to change.

How different that was with the meetings with the managers! The first session was downright dramatic. I had prepared the presentation well; it was absolutely watertight. The story was more detailed than for the employees, and tailored to the behaviour and position of the managers. I felt the climate grow chilly even as I gave the presentation. Countless critical questions and comments came immediately after the presentation: 'Was the research actually based on a representative sample? The questionnaire was biased, that was immediately clear. Were sound analyses performed, since in reality things worked very differently? The research was already three months old, so it was an outdated picture. Were the researchers really independent? The presentation was actually a very academic story.' The more carefully I tried to give an answer, the greater the uproar. We never made it to a discussion.

Looking back at the difference between the meetings with the employees and the first meeting with the managers, it was obvious that an open discussion had arisen with the employees. The post-its contributed to this, but that was not the only thing. The employees recognised themselves in the data and felt acknowledged in their opinions. No discussion came about with the managers. The data was perceived as attacking their role and behaviour and the managers felt that their opinions and experiences were ignored. They felt committed to the company and responsible for how things went there, but no attention at all was paid to that. Instead of an open discussion, it turned into a debate about the objective truth of the research and the research methods. The managers adopted a stance as 'watchmen' of the culture which they had helped design.

I changed my approach for the second meeting with a different group of managers. To start with, the managers were asked what they thought would come out of the research. They worked on that in small groups, and the pictures were presented to each other. After a short break I told them what we had found during our diagnosis. During this story, I gave a global explanation of the similarities we saw with the pictures of the managers and where differences emerged. Then we posed the question whether we could understand the differences together. This meeting went very smoothly. The pictures of the managers were more negative in some aspects than what the diagnosis revealed. Yet other points were confirmed by the outcomes of the diagnosis, with a deepening of what the managers brought forward themselves. The diagnosis was more negative for some points than what the managers themselves experienced daily. The discussion clarified a great deal for the managers but also just as much for me as researcher. There was a climate of equality and space for sharing amazement, expressing emotions and interpreting outcomes. Energy arose for going further.

This experience contains valuable lessons for the diagnosis of organisations. A watertight message allows little space for a real discussion. As a diagnostician you create a defensive climate yourself if you only pay attention to the outcomes you found and you have no attention for the subjective feelings that your story evokes. A one-sided focus on *what* you find ignores *who* is involved and denies the feelings, experiences and ambitions of those people involved. If you consider people as objects, they will behave like subjects: they will talk back. The trick is not to convince others. The skill is in taking people seriously, setting your own truth aside and listening to the perspectives of others. Only then will you achieve an open discussion which creates energy for cooperating on change.

# Imagining
# ambitions

Our preparations for the trip include formulating our ambitions, fantasising about the highlight of the trip, choosing our rest days and discussing the destination where we intend to regain our strength. We form a picture of the landscape and can see the future journey before us already. We are really keen to get going.

# 9
# Urgency and solidarity

*Why urgency arouses paralysis*

Many management books say you have to create a sense
of urgency before people will want to change. The prevailing idea is that people will only want to get moving if they
are under pressure. People have to let go of old certainties
and they need help to do this.

Creating urgency to get others to change is an outmod-
ed idea. Everything is already in motion. Organisations
are changing continuously. One reorganisation is hardly
finished before the next is announced. It is more the case
that the economic malaise has created an excessively
strong awareness of urgency and growing uncertainty so
that paralysis arises and changes stagnate.

The thoughts on urgency are no longer realistic; they
are constructs from the previous century. In those days,
people could stay with the one boss their whole lives,
companies were very inflexible and the organisation
was based predominantly on bureaucratic principles. An
unambiguous hierarchy still existed then, and you listened
to the boss, or at any rate, you pretended to. In those days,
change was a task for managers who did everything they
could to implement changes systematically.

Times have changed. Companies are less rigid than they
used to be. The labour market has become more flexible
than ever, and the number of self-employed people grows
every day. The new way of working results in a greater
distance between company and employee, and sometimes

contributes to alienation. The times we live in are unstable, exciting and challenging. A change planned and imposed from higher up does not suit our times.

It is nonsensical to think that managers have to create a sense of urgency to make changes possible. Of course, if a company is in a crisis it is important to tell how things are, openly and honestly. Leaders will always seize a crisis to push through changes. A crisis situation can be a motive for change, but it is not a necessary first step. A crisis situation in a company often points at failing leadership. Changes in the surroundings are not anticipated by management and arrive as a surprise. Or there is rash investment in expansion or market broadening, which means it is not possible to cope with adverse economic conditions, and creditworthiness is affected. Management targets the short term, leaving insufficient investment in innovation. This brings the product portfolio out of balance and turnover drops. Internal orientation causes contact with the customer to disintegrate and the view of the competition is lost. These four situations do result in crisis and through that, in urgency, but that urgency does not come totally unexpectedly. Management focused excessively on the short term, or simply did not pay attention. Sometimes the management of a company calls too fast and too often that there is a crisis. That suggests more a need to play the hero, or inability of management to make people enthusiastic about trying out new things.

Crisis is not a condition of change. A clear vision of the future is. At least just as essential is the customer value which the company wants to deliver. Companies that are successful in far-reaching changes have a very clear picture of their customers, the needs of these customers and how they can give substance to them. Change is not about organising a crisis, but about organising desire.

But even with organising desire we are not there yet. In uncertain times and with more and more temporary

employment, there is a growing need to belong somewhere. This is not about *'a sense of urgency,'* but about
*'a sense of belonging'*. Organisations with too many
feelings of crisis have a low chance of survival. They go
adrift. These days, it is about creating work communities
in which people have the feeling they belong and make
meaningful contributions. It is about connecting people
so that they can achieve an attractive future together.
Companies with a clear picture of the future and a strong
sense of community have the best survival chances in
uncertain times.

Changing people in organisations is not about articulat-
ing urgency. It is much more about organising desire. This
is perhaps best expressed in the words from *Citadelle* by
Antoine de Saint-Exupéry:

'If you want to build a ship, don't drum up people to
collect wood and don't assign them tasks and work [...],
but rather teach them to long for the endless immensity
of the sea.'

# 10

# Organising desire

*Imagining the future and appreciating
professional pride*

Do you know the Sewer Museum in Paris? You really
should visit it. The entrance is close to Pont de l'Alma.
A drain cover is the opening to the most extraordinary
museum in Paris. You actually go down into the sewer:
you can see it and you can smell it. The Parisian sewer is
the oldest and largest sewerage system in the world. It is
just as big as the street plan of Paris. The whole system is
more than 2,100 kilometres long. There are large pipes with
a diameter of more than five metres, and smaller pipes
of a metre wide and two metres high: you can still walk
through them. The sewer drains all the waste water from
the kitchens and toilets of Paris. And it is also used to drain
rainwater. If the pipes cannot handle the quantity of water,
for instance during rainstorms, the excess rainwater and
waste water flows into the Seine. That is why it is important that sewer workers keep the pipes clean and remove
sludge which cakes up. That allows more water to drain
off. Often the sewer workers stand up to their waists in the
middle of the muck to remove the sludge. It is unattractive
work even though it is essential to keep the city liveable
and healthy. What was something the sewer workers could
be proud of? What was a meaningful strategy here? The
strategy for the sewer work was phrased as follows: *We are
ensuring that salmon will again swim in the Seine in 2010.*
This strategy was motivational, meaningful and quantifiable. It motivated the sewer workers, because they had

the feeling that they were nature conservation managers of the city and contributed in that way to a healthy living climate. It was meaningful, because the strategy made clear what the organisation stood for and what their social contribution was. And it was quantifiable. In fact, salmon did swim again in the Seine for the first time in 2010.

Naturally this result added to the professional pride of the sewer workers. From that feeling of pride, the sewer workers set up their museum themselves, showing how important the maintenance and cleaning is for the health and liveability of a large city like Paris.

You can see professional pride in many people who roll up their sleeves and get to work. They are our rubbish collectors, incinerator operators, bus drivers, engineers, cleaners, road builders, nurses, bricklayers, train drivers, carpenters, plumbers and all people who practise a real trade. Men and women. The people who fulfil an almost invisible role in keeping our society going. They are usually not appreciated enough for their work. Even if it is just to show your appreciation, the sewer museum is worth visiting.

The professional pride of people is an important source of energy for result and renewal. In most railway companies, the professional knowledge of the personnel on the trains is valued highly. The train drivers and conductors form the heart of the service to customers, and they are a connecting link with the complicated logistical process underlying the way the trains run. A new training centre has been built for the train drivers, including the latest simulation technology. Train drivers meet each other in this environment and exchange experiences so they can improve the service. In simulation trains they learn how to work with new equipment and they gain experience in unexpected situations which can endanger the safety and the timetable. It is about making professional pride visible and acknowledging it, and about encouraging safety and a service-oriented nature. Appreciating professional pride contributes to company pride. It also leads to new initiatives, such as the establishment of a 'guild of conductors and train drivers' whose ambition is to improve the service from the members' professionalism and company pride.

In hospitals too, professional pride is a driving force for improving patient care. A good example of this is the *Appraisal & Assessment* programme which was established by a few doctors. Peer review is used to raise the quality of the medical specialists. A colleague collects information about how a doctor functions from patients, nursing staff, doctors in training and colleagues. Each discussion partner formulates three good points and three tips for improvement of the professional's behaviour. This information is discussed in a peer meeting. The experiences are conclusive. Besides boosting the cooperation between colleagues and improving the individual professional acting, this impressive method of peer review is of most benefit to the patients.

Innovation often originates from professional pride and the elusive knowledge of the staff carrying out the work. Managers can sometimes forget that the company would come to a standstill without the workers performing the work. In the end, company results are achieved by people who serve customers daily and roll up their sleeves. Many board members and staff specialists cannot imagine that the staff performing the work are capable of realising innovations. Renewal often arises on the shop floor and comes from people who are proud of their profession, who roll up their sleeves and who dare to experiment.

# 11
# Doing business together

*Why ready-made solutions often result in problems*

A few years ago senior civil servants in the Dutch Minis-
try of Security and Justice took an initiative. Too many cases were disappearing unnoticed in the criminal justice system. And that started with the police. If the police made a mistake in a criminal law investigation, the chance of getting a suspect sentenced was quickly lost. Further on in the chain the coordination was not flawless either. The waiting time between bringing and preparing a case and its handling by public prosecutors and courts was far too long. Cases piled up. The probation service could hardly keep up when suspects reoffended. They had incomplete files for many multiple offenders. And far too often people from the Child Care and Protection Board did not turn up at court hearings. Too many cases were dismissed. Something had to happen to coordinate the work better. So a decision was made to introduce a system for planning and control. But none of the professionals in the criminal justice system saw any good in it. There was resistance. What now?

The ministry had taken the initiative for the new system. The public administration system and the IT department took the lead. But now that it was time for implementation, none of the chain partners wanted to cooperate. The courts invoked their legal independence: they did not want to be checked. The public prosecutors did not want to be crammed into a planning straitjacket. And the people from

55

the probation service and child protection didn't believe
in it. It was all far too technical and did not do the clients
any justice. How should we proceed from here? Push it
through? Enforce it? Explain it yet again?

The solution was eventually as simple as it was effective.
While the executive support department did have a solution, the problem was not shared. A number of sessions
were used to bring people together who had different tasks
in the criminal justice system. Three simple questions
were posed in these sessions: what does your work look

like and what do you do? What kinds of problems do you
come across in your work? This made it clear for everyone
what the problems were in the criminal justice system.
People were very amazed by the problems and recognised
how those problems were reproduced day after day. Once
the problems were shared, the third question could be
asked: why can't we keep on going the same way? That
question resulted in vehement, emotional reactions: 'It's
about the legitimacy of our legal system,' 'If we don't take
offenders to court, what does that mean for the victims?,'
'It really is disgraceful that we all make such a mess of it'
and 'It's about safety in neighbourhoods and districts, that
is what we stand for.' In the discussions, which were often
heated, it became clear that some kind of coordination
was required in the criminal justice system. It concerned
the right of existence of the judicial system. It was about
justice in the neighbourhood. Now the time was ripe for
the fourth question: what can we do?

The answers to the fourth question were striking: almost
all the groups came up with the suggestion of developing
an information system to coordinate the tasks. But extra
ideas turned up as well. 'If it is about safety in the neighbourhoods and districts, why don't we just go and work
together with those neighbourhoods and districts?' And
thus the policy initiative 'Justice in the Neighbourhood'
came about. Experiments with local collaboration were

done in neighbourhoods. This collaboration in the neighbourhood was not limited to people from the Department of Justice. Youth care and social work joined in as well. The addiction services wanted to participate as well, as did debt management services and the housing corporation. Institutional barriers at a local level vanished into thin air. There was a great deal of enthusiasm for cooperation, and the safety in the neighbourhoods increased noticeably.

'What a great solution for the problems in the chain. If we could just make this a *best practice*,' the people from the public administration system at the ministry thought. A solution was subsequently set out in more detail to roll out across the rest of the country. And again there was resistance from the people the solution was intended for. The positive development came to an abrupt standstill, except in the neighbourhoods where the people themselves had taken the lead and saw the positive results. Further implementation stagnated. Or did it?

People who were enthusiastic about their experiences went out to tell their stories. They got colleagues in nearby neighbourhoods enthusiastic, and they were willing to share their experiences. Quite soon it emerged that each neighbourhood needed a different approach and had its own set of partners, and that building cooperation was without doubt a condition of success. The initiatives shot up like mushrooms. It seemed to be a spontaneous process over which the ministry had no control. But you would do best not to call it Justice in the Neighbourhood. That term had become tainted. 'System justice', or 'Safety house', maybe. And really, the name didn't matter all that much. The point was that the initiative contributed to safer neighbourhoods and districts.

This experience contains a number of fascinating learning experiences. If you want to achieve a change, it is best to share the problem and not turn up with a ready-made solution. And take care with standardisation and rolling out successful practices. If you deny local conditions, enthusiasm and creativity, you have already organised your own resistance.

# 12
# Pictures of the future

*If you agree about the future, the rest will take care of itself*

Nobody expected that there was a future for the cooperation between KLM and Air France. There are few successful
mergers between French and Dutch companies: the
cultural differences between the two countries are simply
too large. The people at KLM are proud of their company
and they feel a strong bond with it. When the cooperation
with Air France was announced, the KLM people took a
wait-and-see approach. 'I didn't really have a picture of Air
France, but I did have an idea about the French in general:
they're chauvinistic and they want to act the boss. I was
afraid of that in the beginning.'
   What made the cooperation a success and what can we
learn from that?

It started with the two CEOs, Leo van Wijk of KLM and
Jean-Cyril Spinetta of Air France. They knew each other
from the International Air Transport Association: they
were both on the board. They had the same vision of the
future of aviation, in which cooperation is essential to
international operations and keeping ahead of low-cost
carriers and new rivals from emerging economies like
China and the Arab countries. The starting principle of
the cooperation between KLM and Air France is equality.
Spinetta: 'Right from the start, I cannot recall any instance
of a significant disagreement between us about the strategy for the group.' Both men invested a great deal in their

relationship with each other and they treated each other in a friendly manner. What's more, the two senior executives were not obstructed by their own egos: 'Who would be number one and who would be number two, we never had that kind of problem.' In their numerous appearances about the cooperation, Spinetta and Van Wijk always presented themselves together and had an equal amount of speaking time, and they displayed their friendship ostentatiously. KLM and Air France were displayed in equal ratio in the background, and both KLM and Air France airplane models graced the table in front of them. Equality was highlighted in word and image.

The new company's course of action was clear: offer passengers the most destinations worldwide, with no more than one transfer. Air France and KLM chose a strategy which was based on clear customer values: reliability, ease and comfort for a competitive price. The vision for the organisation was also exceedingly clear: *'One company, two airlines, three businesses.'* The *company* was the holding Air France and KLM. The two *airlines* were KLM and Air France which each retained their own identity. The *three businesses* referred to passenger transport, freight transport and maintenance. From the start, it was agreed that *'fairness'* would form the leading principle in the cooperation. The action was suited to the word, because even though the ownership structure of Air France is four times larger than that of KLM, the seats on the Board of Directors were shared equally: four for people from Air France and four for people from KLM. There is ongoing investment in the hub airports and networks of both airlines. The principle is that integration only takes place if there are good reasons for that. Many activities continue to be controlled independently by each airline.

Another interesting perspective was chosen in the cooperation: the one party is not in essence better than the other – the essence is that you can learn from each other and together you can perform better. Thus Spinetta presented KLM Cargo as a fantastic cargo company and he invited the people of Air France to go and take a look around there and learn from it. Van Wijk in turn appreciated Air France's service for passengers during the flight, and he invited the cabin crew of KLM to learn from it.

It worked. In 2012 KLM received a prize for the best in-flight service in Europe. The ambition for the future is clear: become the best airline for reliability, sustainability and service. This ambition is inspiring for many staff members and provides a direction.

Several initiatives were undertaken to make cultural differences visible and open to discussion. Culture workshops were offered to people who would have to deal with their merger partner in practice and directly. Joint training sessions and management meetings helped people to get to know each other and learn from each other. One fascinating initiative was the exchange programme for Young Executives. Ten promising talented people from KLM went to Air France in Paris and ten talented people from Air France went to the headquarters of KLM to work on integration projects. These people were asked to keep a diary of stories about their experiences and the things that had surprised them during this exchange. At the end of their exchange period they worked together and collected their stories in a book. The book gives a fantastic insight into the curious customs in both companies and into the cultural differences which could result in misunderstandings.

By making unsaid expectations and cultural habits explicit, misunderstandings can be avoided and you can laugh about the idiosyncrasies in your company and accept the idiosyncrasies of your colleagues at the merger partner's company.

The experiences in the cooperation between KLM and Air France provide countless lessons. Possibly the most important lesson is that a clear and meaningful picture of the future generates confidence in the change. It is essential to get the meaning of the merger for the customer straight right away. Justice is a basic principle, as is the willingness to learn from each other in order to strengthen each other and improve together. And of course, exemplary behaviour by top management is crucial for credibility. A joint ambition and clear pictures of the future get people moving, all the more so if top management radiates community spirit and trust.

# Travelling in the unknown

Once we have formed a good picture of the area and the destination, we choose a possible route and make agreements with the people who are going on this adventure with us. We work out what kinds of materials and provisions we need on our trip and estimate whether there is enough water along the way. We map out the route and get going, well prepared.

# 13

# A good idea is dangerous

*About ideology, sense of direction and flexibility*

'My name is Ronald Bell and I am the manager of a credit card company. I have a fantastic idea for setting up my organisation differently. Could I invite you to come and talk about this idea with me?' The email text was brief and to the point and I was curious.

The office of the credit card company was located in cheerless surroundings. The office building itself was typically seventies style. That made the interior all the more surprising, with its contemporary, colourful design furniture, conversation corners and an open reception area. Ronald bounded down the stairs to greet me personally. 'It's great you've come! I want to put something to you.'

Even before I had hung up my coat, Ronald fired away. 'I read this amazing book: *Maverick*. It is about a company in Brazil where the employees organise everything themselves. That motivates them so much that high productivity goes hand-in-hand with a lot of pleasure in their work. I went to a convention where the whole concept was explained. And then I went and visited the Semco company myself. It really is impressive. I think it would be wonderful to introduce that here too.'

I was familiar with the book *Maverick*. The Brazilian company Ronald mentioned produces cement agitators and ignores all kinds of established principles. There are no fixed working hours in the company. The employees decide themselves how much they earn, they select and assess their boss themselves and financial information is available for everyone. The productivity is high and large profits are made.

I felt a bit overwhelmed by Ronald's uncontrolled energy. Semco style in a credit card company? I wondered whether that was such a good idea. 'I understand you are enthusiastic about the ideas of Ricardo Semler and that you are considering implementing his ideas here too.'

The answer was not long in coming: 'Oh definitely, I think it would be tremendous. That would make things quieter for me too, and as a company we could work more efficiently. And we need that, because right now we are too expensive as a credit card company.'

My reaction was brief: 'I wonder whether it is such a good idea. Why are you too expensive now as a company?'

I didn't get a direct answer to this question, except that introducing this Semco style 'would solve all the problems'.

Ronald's answer to my question about what others in the company thought about it was: 'Oh, nobody likes change, you know that best. A few people are really enthusiastic, just like me. I would really dare to do it, with them. And the people who don't want to join in can just leave. You have to believe in it, and if you don't, you simply don't work with us any more. Can you help me introduce this concept?'

'I don't believe it is a good idea to introduce this style just like that. Your company cannot afford to take any risks in the handling of money flows. If you are too expensive now, you would probably benefit more from standardising and computerising the work processes. I don't think it is wise to introduce the new work concept from the top of the organisation through the company. You argue for a democratic working method, but you want to impose the implementation on others from the top down. What will you do if most of your employees leave?'

After this critical note, the discussion came to an end swiftly.

It is remarkable that managers can sometimes believe in their own or other people's ideas so much that they only seek confirmation of their own ideas. You can always find that confirmation from about five percent of the employees. They are the followers; the people who don't dare contradict you and are keen to climb higher. So that's useless to you. The trick is to find those employees who recognise the problems and want to work on them. These employees are usually experienced staff members and committed to the company. They represent about 15 percent of the employees in a company. Their commitment pushes them to ask critical questions. Ronald had found his allies in the followers. His single-mindedness would have alienated the other employees from him. I warned Ronald that his dream would end in failure and that *Maverick* may be a nice story, but not a good idea for a credit card company with financial problems.

Ronald did not push his idea further. Once he hit a wall of incomprehension, he tackled things more cautiously. He achieved a reliable and efficient credit card company with a well-thought-out change process. Then he changed jobs. I recently received an email from him: 'Jaap, now I am working for a company that makes industrial doors. I have a really great idea and I have already got a long way with the realisation. Would you like to come and talk about it with me? I want to show you something...'

A good idea is dangerous, especially if you only have one. And that is definitely the case if that idea comes from a manager or client and it is not in keeping with the assignment, the work processes of the company and the problems in the company. Change starts with standing still. What is the essence of the problem? Who can help in tackling the problem? Which solutions are possible and which solution is the most desirable? How will we design the change? If a leader or manager threatens to head off in the wrong direction, it is the duty of the supervisor, colleague or advisor to enter into discussion with him/her and not to avoid the conflict. It can help to ask which problem this idea is meant to solve. Change is about the future of the company and not about a tempting ideology or the glory of people at the top.

# 14
# Synergy

*How vague projects contribute to uncertainty and arguments*

I received a call from a senior civil servant in a certain ministry. Two ministries had been merged into a single ministry. The senior political body wanted synergy. Their idea was that maybe this could be achieved in the business operations. It seemed to be simplest to merge the two IT departments. A policy document was written, a synergy programme was started and a project leader was appointed to make sure everything ran smoothly.

'We started in good spirits,' said the senior civil servant. 'And we really worked very carefully,' added the project leader whose job it was to realise that synergy between the IT departments. 'We got people involved in it, set up work-groups, made lists of the tasks, asked for suggestions. But when it came to the point, all kinds of conflicts emerged. The whole process stalled. Now, we heard that you can fix up change processes which have become stuck.' They looked at me expectantly.

Hmm, what do you do in this kind of case? My answer was that I would like to have a look at what was going on, but that I had no idea whether I could be of service to them. They gave me the space to go out and investigate. The first thing to do was to visit the two workgroup leaders.

'Of course you've been sent by the top to reorganise things here,' was what I heard from the first workgroup leader after I had introduced myself.

'Well, not really,' was my answer. 'They did ask me to, but I have no idea what is happening and whether I can do anything meaningful. Perhaps you can help by telling me what is going on.'

After some hesitation I was given the benefit of the doubt. 'Yes, we were forced into this synergy, but it's only turning into a mess. Two workgroups were formed, one from each ministry. They were instructed to find out which system was best for the ministry, since there was going to be just one system: those were the orders. My workgroup came to the conclusion that the AS400 system was the best. It has enormous computing power and we need that so we can steer all the subsidy schemes in the right direction. But then there are those 'Apes & Idiots'... Sorry, the guys from Automation & Informatics, the department from the other ministry, they just don't understand anything about it and they went for the system from Digital. Well, it escalated. Now we don't talk with each other any more, since all we do is fight.'

My meeting with the second workgroup leader also got off to an unusual start. 'Oh, here we go, yet another advisor who has come to line his pockets,' was the opening sentence when I introduced myself.

Surprised, I answered: 'Gee, I guess your experiences with advisors haven't been all that good: want to tell me about it?'

I was steered into the room with a roar of laughter. 'Well, it has really got out of hand. We all started quite well. Both workgroups made good lists of the core tasks of the ministry and how they could be supported by IT. In my workgroup we argued for the Digital system, since it is much more capable of supporting the policy functions, and that's what it's all about here, since we are a policy department. Well, then suddenly the people from the other workgroup were calling us Apes & Idiots. Their own department used to be called Information & Automation.

So it didn't take long for members from my workgroup to call them Imbecile & Arrogant. We haven't talked with each other since then.'

It looked like the issue was completely deadlocked. What was the reason for choosing one single system? Why were the workgroups formed along the lines of the former departments? Merge the departments? Why? Why was optimum support of the core tasks, which were very different, not the basis? Where did the idea come from that cutbacks were possible if all the tasks continued to exist? What did synergy actually mean? I went back to the senior civil servant and the programme leader with these questions. My questions embarrassed them. 'Yes, it was the political top who demanded synergy. Doesn't that mean merging, reorganisations, cutting costs? And surely that would only be possible by having a single system...'

The programme was pushed aside, the workgroups were disbanded, and the idea that a single system had to be selected was dropped. Both systems were necessary so that the core functions received optimum support. A challenging learning project was established for people from both IT departments. Inspiring speakers and top experts set to work with the IT professionals to explore the possibilities for renewal. This led to initiatives for improving the services. Gradually trust was created again. People participating in the learning project then got busy on realising the improvements. Knowledge was combined, cooperation with the users was established, and renewals were implemented. The IT professionals became interested in both systems. Little by little, synergy acquired meaning. It was about better service, about innovation, about combining forces. It was not about choosing a single system or about savings and cutbacks. Synergy was created through the exchange of knowledge, appreciation for the professionals and through appealing to their power for renewal.

I learned a great deal from this adventure. Watch out if the objectives for a change have been laid down in a policy document and a project has been started without regard for the issues and the context. Vague concepts such as synergy or renewal result in vague assignments, misunderstanding and uncertainty. Paralysis and quarrels are the consequence. Changes fail if the core tasks are neglected and ambitions are unclear. With change it is at the very least about why the change is desirable, what the change should contribute to, and where the change will lead. If people meet each other and are no longer strangers to each other, they automatically become curious about the other. Curiosity to discover other people's worlds is a fantastic seedbed for change.

# 15

# Reasoned resistance

*Taking others' experiences seriously*

Designing an organisation is a process involving much
deliberation. A good design starts by identifying and listing
the customer processes. Customer processes start with
a question or requirement of a customer and end with
services or products which are delivered to the customer.
You want to handle customer questions as best as possible: rapidly, faultlessly, in a customer-oriented way and
economically. Once you know the customer processes,
you find out the best way to set them up, how you organise
the coordination of the work, how you design the hierarchy and how you match up the technical systems.

A company which processed funds transfers decided
on a drastic renewal of its administrative systems. This
technical innovation would bring significant changes to
the work of the people in the company. The organisation
of the work and the control structure thus also had to
be modified. A challenging task, so I got cracking. First I
identified and listed all the customers with their specific
demands. All the banks in the country were customers of
the company. The banks supplied payment data which
had to be processed as soon as possible. That processing
was a job which had to be done with the utmost precision.
Around four billion went through the organisation every
day, and you didn't want any money to go astray or the
payment transactions in the country to shut down. After

the customer processes, I also gathered information about the products. There were quite a lot of them: transfers, disks with salary payments, mortgage payments, bank card payments, credit card transactions. Of course, with the new design I also took the locations of the company into consideration, as well as logistics and transport, the new technology which was being developed and the quality of the work. I was rather pleased with the wonderful design of the organisation which came out.

I very proudly presented the new organisational design to the board members. They thought it was splendid. 'An excellent well-thought-out design and it simplifies the control considerably.' The new work organisation had been built from customer demands and appropriate technology. Thus a distinction was made between company processes for salary payments, mortgages, automatic payments and so on.

The middle managers were less enthusiastic. 'Yes, look, you're the one who has studied to do this kind of thing, and if you think it will work, then you'll just have to do it.' There were no real objections, but the atmosphere was resigned.

Then I went to the employees. That was where commotion arose: 'This is really a very stupid plan,' was the immediate response to my presentation. 'No, that won't work at all, you can see that straight away.' Many managers and advisors would regard this as resistance to change which you should oppose. Luckily I kept on asking questions about their objections. 'When does your salary come through?' they asked me. 'Ah, usually in the third week of the month.' 'Yes, it's the same for everyone else as well. And when do you pay your rent or mortgage?' 'As late as possible of course, so usually the last week of the month,' I answered. 'Yes, and that's how the rest of the customers do it too. And have you ever looked when most pay orders come in to be processed?'

The design had taken everything into account, except

the peak moments in the work. The proposed setup would mean that the one department would have a peak load in the third week of the month, the other in the fourth week and yet another department would have a peak load in the first week. And that meant that processing within the specified time could not be guaranteed. I had to make significant modifications to my design, thanks to the employees who knew their own work processes through and through. Apparently the board members did not have that understanding of the work processes. They were mainly charmed by the simplicity of the control which would make their own work easier. The middle managers kept out of it and did not want to burn their fingers on a conflict with the board or be accused of resisting change. The employees were committed to their work and they had the best understanding of the possible consequences from the perspective of the customer.

If major changes are concerned, it is wise to make use of the knowledge and experience of the employees involved in the customer and work processes. Support from management does not guarantee that the new design of the organisation is right. Today, it is sensible to find out where resistance comes from. People can sometimes be against change because it threatens their position. Their behaviour is a reaction to actions by others who usually do not suffer from them themselves. More frequently, people are uncertain because the communication about the change is not done well. Their reservations are a reaction to stupid handling by change managers. People generally want to participate in thinking about a change. That they don't always agree to a new plan is not a sign of resistance, but of commitment. The employees in this company were not displaying resistance, but common sense. It is best to take that common sense seriously.

## 16

# What am I doing wrong that makes him so mad?

*About self-reflection, appreciation and trust*

There is always tension between continuity and renewal. Continuity is founded on well-beaten tracks, rules and routines. It concerns the exploitation of existing knowledge and routines. With exploitation, people strive for security and efficiency. Exploitation stabilises. When services, products or work methods are renewed, what is involved is exploration. With exploration, people look for renewal. Exploitation calls the existing situation into question. Exploration disrupts it.

The tension between exploration and exploitation was not as self-evident a few years back. The management board of a financial institution had asked me to design a process of renewal. The system for funds transfers had to be renewed. That entailed the modification of the workflows and the structure as well. I had the lovely task of supervising the process of renewal.

　　The process of renewal proceeded quite well. The business processes had been analysed meticulously and redesigned. The development of the new technical systems was in full swing and the contours of the new organisation began to take shape. The board supported the new plans, as did the works council which understood the necessity of the changes. Only Pete, the manager of funds transfer operations, continually brought the innovation plans up for discussion. He was such a conservative person. He didn't want to hear about change. I thought he was not a good manager, because if you're managing stagnation you do nothing except sit on your hands. Ultimately this was about the management of change. And Pete wanted nothing to do with that.

This manager was actually a risk for the project. One day when I was cycling home from work, I started thinking: what makes him so mad? As I cycled I went over the project again. Nothing seemed to be wrong with the structure, and the new system seemed to be in order. Those four billion guilders should get through it every day without any problems. I was suddenly seized by a sinking feeling: four billion a day! What would happen if the funds transfers in our country broke down?

Pete had ensured undisturbed funds transfers for twenty years now. Every day four billion guilders went through a complicated system of information flows without a single flaw. In all those years he had met all timelines and had not lost a single cent. And then I came along, an external project leader who only thought about renewal and had little awareness of the vulnerability of the funds transfers. I should have been asking myself: 'What am I doing wrong that makes him so mad?'

The next day, at the end of the afternoon, I reluctantly turned up at Pete's office. 'Ah, Pete, can I have a word with you?'

'Yes, take a seat,' answered Pete, without taking his eyes off his work.

'Well, ah, I was thinking about that whole renewal thing again, and… it is a very big risk, because if the funds transfers fail then we really have a problem.'

Pete looked up, amazed, and after a deep sigh he said: 'Well… Finally you've realised that, laddie?'

'Hmm, yes. And I believe I underestimated that risk,' I answered, embarrassed.

'You certainly did, and the disaster would have been incalculable if things had gone wrong.'

It was clear that Pete had an opinion about me too: 'Hotshot from Amsterdam,' he told me later. I personified the exploration and renewal. Pete was the exploitation: stability and continuity. We couldn't do without each other: we needed each other. And that is how it went. We worked together on the renewal of the funds transfers: Pete with his eye for stability and continuity, and me with

my focus on new possibilities. A new payment system came and a new work organisation was introduced. The funds transfer was not down for a single day, and not a single cent was lost. Thanks to Pete.

This adventure contains many learning experiences: the tension between exploration and exploitation can be put to use to realise renewals and simultaneously avoid risks and guarantee continuity. You need trust to make use of that tension. You have to work on that. When building trust, it is easier to change your own behaviour than to force others to change theirs. In order to avoid swift judgements and work on mutual trust, it is best to ask yourself: 'What am I doing wrong that makes him so mad?'

# Tackling the unexpected

During the hike we keep an eye on the weather conditions and we watch out for each other. Unexpected things always happen. The stream is wilder than we thought and it is hardly possible to ford it at the point we had intended. The weather suddenly changes and it is too risky to continue walking. The descent turns out to be steeper than we thought, and one of us doesn't dare to do it.

# 17
# Culture change

*Why it's better if not everyone thinks the same*

Announcing a culture change can appear to be the solution to many problems. There is a need to set a new and
clear direction with core values to change behaviour and
everybody has to think the same. That solves all your problems just like that.

De Nederlandsche Bank (the Dutch National Bank) lost its
social legitimacy following the problems in the financial
sector and with some banks that had to be saved, pushing
the minister to rush headlong into change. A new action
plan for a culture change was required within two months.
When the railways had to increase its customer focus
following its privatisation, management initiated a cultural programme. When patients stayed away from a certain
hospital, the Board of Directors started a cultural project.
Obviously cultural programmes are popular among minis-
ters and managers who believe that others have to change.
   Cultural change is one of the most frequently
mentioned and one of the most difficult ways of improving the way an organisation functions. One of the reasons
why it is so difficult to change an organisational culture is
that the prevailing values and norms in the organisation
are so robust. You cannot change entrenched patterns
just like that. An announced cultural change often results
in uncertainty for employees. The announcement of
a cultural change makes clear to them at any rate that

their behaviour is not right and that they have to change. Managers often have trouble with cultural change because they helped create that culture themselves. They are the embodiment of the culture and it is not easy to cut into your own body.

The presentation of the plan for the cultural change at De Nederlandsche Bank kept the minister out of the firing line for a while. This kind of programme takes a good two years, and that provides good possibilities for avoiding flak. Eighteen months later there was another uproar, this time concerning state aid for another bank. The plan for the cultural change had not yet borne fruit, but a great deal of work was being put into it. Moreover, this was for cultural change, and you can't change a culture just like that.

Following the merger of two hospitals, the Supervisory Board of the new hospital started a cultural change programme. It got off to a good start. The new name of the hospital was announced at a big celebration. A communal vision was formulated at a conference with management. All means of communication were used to put the spotlight on that vision. The new identity was already visible in the new company style. The new structure was there. But the cooperation between specialists did not get off the ground, and the tension between doctors and nursing staff grew. Conflicts arose between the medical specialists and the Supervisory Board. The Supervisory Board went even further. Everybody had to think the same way and cultural sessions were intended to help achieve this. The process stalled. In the corridors it became apparent that nobody had confidence any more that the change would succeed. But then a work conference was arranged with the members of the Supervisory Board and the medical staff with the theme: 'How can we trust each other and how can we work with each other.' Suddenly it became possible to discuss the non-discussable. Cultural change was not mentioned at all. It was about the care for the patients, day in, day out. Initiatives by nursing and medical staff arose from the grassroots level to make tangible improvements to the care. Looking back, the board chairman concluded: 'Culture is behaviour and never a goal in itself. It is about quality of the daily care processes. If that happens properly, you will get there without having to apply force.'

Cultural programmes which target nothing other than behavioural change are senseless. Cultural change does not succeed with a planned approach and control imposed from above. If everybody thinks the same, variation is destroyed and oppressive group thinking is cultivated. That makes change increasingly difficult. Companies that have success with cultural change never call it cultural change and they do not hide it away in a programme. Culture is rooted in the daily work and in opinions of how you do your work, in a vision and in a clear concept of service. Leaders in cultural change give direction, create space and demand results. If you take the cultural experiences of others seriously, the culture will change gradually and step by step without any need to pull, push or force.

## 18

# Destruction

*Breaking new ground fearlessly*

84 The training programme for organisational advisors
needed renewal. At least, that is what I thought when I
was appointed Chancellor of an inter-university Centre
for Development in Organisational Studies and Change
Management. The programme had been running successfully for years. And yet to my mind it no longer catered
for contemporary insights in the field of organisational
advice. The question thrust itself on me: was it still possible
to define the advisor of the future in generic attainment
targets? A second question was whether consultation
work would only be performed by respectable agencies.
Or would advisors become more independent and build
up networks around specific assignments? These doubts
about the future of organisational advisors led to several ambitious questions: could a programme be made for
top advisors which did justice to the diversity of advisors?
Could a programme be developed which accepted a broad
knowledge base and played with it?

Enthusiastic about the new possibilities, I entered into
discussions with the teachers of the existing programme.
Quite quickly it became clear that my enthusiasm was
not shared. The existing programme was considered to
be the flagship of the institute, at any rate by the teachers
who played a role in it. Together those teachers formed a
strong team, and because of that, they were a team with
power. They tolerated few other people and certainly no

different opinions. Moreover, the teachers were convinced that the course was unique. We had many debates about the future of the profession and its meaning for the programme, but they led to little clarity. The renewal was completely stuck.

What do you do as leader if you are convinced that renewal is necessary, while the parties who are directly involved do not want to enter into a discussion on the subject, turn their back on other perspectives and do not tolerate people with different opinions and experiences? A fixation on the contents developed, because the discussion stalled, and a social stagnation developed because other people and points of view were not permitted. In those kinds of situations you can try to introduce different external approaches, or go and have a look somewhere else. If that does not succeed, you can always make the process discussable and see whether you can realise space for renewal that way. But if the content of the game is not discussable, people do not want to enter any other playing field, the game rules cannot be discussed and people do not want to play any other game, there is only one option left: intervene and switch players.

After twelve months I had had enough. Not only did the redesign not get a step further, the numbers of participants were also dropping. Something had to happen. In the end I decided to stop the course and disband the team. The flagship was destroyed to give a new design and a new team a chance. This was a solid decision founded on ambition. It was also a bit of a naïve decision. I myself thought that we could realise a new programme in nine months. That turned out to be much too optimistic. It took eighteen months to design a properly thought-out learning process and build a new team. No money came in during the redesign, while we continued to incur costs. I learned a relevant lesson from this: innovation costs time and money, and if you first wreak destruction, then the creation process takes longer.

Something else was at play too: the existing course enjoyed a strong reputation. Many advisors derived their own reputation from this course. By destroying this activity, a part of their own identity and reputation was taken from them. I had failed to see that. We had paid specific attention to communication to teachers and market parties, but not to former participants. And they had been well trained, so they made themselves heard. A second lesson could be learned from this: professionals identify with their profession. They derive their identity and security from it. You can never deny that commitment and emotion.

The new top programme for organisational advisors was realised in one-and-a-half years and to my knowledge it is one of the most advanced training programmes for advisors available. I sometimes wonder whether I would have had the courage for destructive renewal if I had foreseen the costs of the investment. Sometimes I think it is better to rely on your intuition and your ambition without being guided too much by numbers. But the most important lesson is that you only achieve real innovation by destroying the existing, even if what already exists is successful. You need courage for that, and optimism. And a certain degree of naivety, because you can only arrive at something entirely new by being fearless.

## 19
# Do it the right way or do the right thing?

*Showing your nerve by choosing new paths*

The majority of children in our Western societies are doing well. A small number of children have problems. That is when help is needed. There are countless agencies in the Netherlands that offer help to children and their parents. The care providers in these organisations do their utmost to give these young people a future.

Anthony is seven years old. At home his mother abuses him. His father left them ages ago. When Anthony is fifteen, he is brought in for vandalism and shoplifting and sent to a reformatory. The reformatory did not stimulate him to learn. When he is sixteen he stops going to school and starts working for cash in hand. Anthony had started smoking cannabis at the reformatory. Two years later he uses hard drugs and he is apprehended again for shoplifting. When he is twenty, Anthony is given accommodation in a supervised residential environment. One year later he is convicted of shoplifting with violence and is sent to a youth prison. A few months later he is back on the streets. Then years of offences and shoplifting follow. When Anthony is twenty-six he is locked up for six months. After that the welfare services really get moving. The probation service monitors him, he is sent to training courses, he is included in a project for supervised residence and a psychiatrist is assigned to him. And yet it goes wrong again and he is caught again and given a prison sentence.

When he comes out of prison there are numerous supervisory officers, practitioners, law enforcement officers and
aid workers taking care of him. It goes all right for a little
while, but then he falls back into drug abuse and theft. In
the end he commits suicide.

The story of Anthony is the story of a frequent offender
who was not capable of getting his own life in order. From
the age of seven to the age of thirty, Anthony had to deal
with sixty professionals from eighteen different author-

ities. Sixty social workers were not able to give a child of
seven a future. And yet they all did their best. The social
worker saw Anthony as a person requesting help and
gave immediate care. For the psychiatrist, Anthony was a
patient who should have made it through treatment and
medicine. The police saw him as a disorderly person who
was in breach of the law. The prosecutor saw Anthony as
a repeat offender who had to be coerced and compelled
to get on the right path, and the courts saw him as a guilty
party who had to be placed in detention. And Anthony? He
increasingly lost the grip on his own life. All the professionals really made the maximum effort and took care of
Anthony. They observed the protocols and followed the
rules. They did it the right way.

Marian is a guardian. She regularly visits John's family and
his little brother Martin. John is allowed to live at home
again after he had been removed because it was unsafe
at home. As guardian, Marian keeps an eye on how John
is doing. During one of her home visits she notices that
Martin seems to be withdrawn. But she is not there for
Martin. And yet it keeps haunting her. She goes to Martin's
primary school teacher and hears that Martin is increasingly withdrawn in the classroom and has concentration
problems. The sports teacher tells her that Martin has
many bruises. The family doctor tells her he cannot tell her

anything due to medical confidentiality, but he recommends that she take action. But what can she do? She does not have guardianship of Martin, and reporting it to the child abuse hotline takes too long for her liking. She consults with the school teacher. Together they talk with parents of the friends of Martin and John, and they ask whether the two brothers can come and stay for a while. That is fine, and thus the two boys go and stay with their friends at their home. Things start going better for Martin and John quite fast. And yet Marian did not do this the right way.

Marian removed two children from parental authority. She took two children to a family which was not even a foster family. She acted without indication or court order. She did not observe the protocols and she broke rules. She exceeded her authority.

Martin and John are still doing well. They continue to live with their friends and a visiting arrangement has been organised with their parents. Marian was tremendously pleased when Martin recently told her: 'Do you know what I'm going to be when I grow up? I'm going to study social work, just like you!' Thinking back over the past years, she knows: I did the right thing.

It is a difficult choice: follow protocols or break rules and overstep your bounds. Many professionals choose the safe path and are supported in that by their managers, their administrators and their supervisors. Other professionals do not want to take the beaten track, but search out new paths. They choose to do the right thing. People who do the right thing are guided by the result: seeing the future in the eyes of children again. You need guts for that, and professional maturity.

To remain true as a professional, it is best to follow your passion and profession. People who take the initiative based on this passion so they can realise renewal deserve the support of administrators, politicians, policymakers and their own managers. A key question for leaders and managers is: do you dare to provide enough space so that professionals can do the right thing?

## 20

# Agility

*About foresight and strategic action*

The sudden 20 percent decline in sales did not come as a surprise. Hans had already seen the crisis coming in the painting branch. As director of a paint wholesaler he knew that the economic crisis would not spare him: 'It was to be expected. If there is a financial crisis in America, that affects the real economy, there's no way around it. And an economic crisis in North America spreads to Europe, that's logical with the way economic activities are interconnected worldwide these days. An economic crisis deeply affects the construction sector first, since less money is available for long-term investments. Moreover, that financial crisis started with the housing market, what do you expect? It is not a question of whether the painting branch will be affected, but when, how severely and how long it will last. But you can see it coming, years in advance, and in that case you can make sure you are ready for it.'

Many entrepreneurs and managers of companies are less alert when a crisis presents itself. Then they are not ready for it and there are few options left open to them for enterprising strategic action. Managers often panic if a crisis also affects their company. The usual strategy is to cut costs. It starts with the training budget, then the marketing budget follows, then there is an attempt to make production cheaper, after which loss-making company activities are divested, and finally staff are sacked. If you don't look ahead, then probably there is little else you can do other than resort to cost cutting. That might seem to be the shortest way to recovery, but often it is a dead end.

Hans did look ahead and he chose a different strategy. He chose for market-oriented acting.

That meant: being aware of what was going on in the market, not panicking, being flexible, targeting the customer and surroundings, keeping his eyes open and seizing opportunities.

The first step was to build a strong financial position so that the company could cope with difficult circumstances. As a major shareholder Hans had already relinquished dividend payments to himself, and he had asked the other major shareholders to follow his example. Then he entered into discussions with the paint manufacturer and bargained for the prices of the paint supplies not to rise, even though the raw materials had become more expensive. His offer was to do business together and be ready for the painters' businesses, on the premise that faithful customers are worth their weight in gold, especially in times of crisis. While other paint manufacturers and paint wholesalers raised their prices, Hans kept them stable. That was how he acquired new customers. While other paint wholesalers limited their credit options, Hans offered faithful customers more financial space. That was how he made friends.

A second step was to continue to invest in customer relations and innovations. European regulations specify that solvent-based paints are forbidden in favour of water-based paints. The vendors knew that painters were sceptical and rejected the use of water-based paints. On the basis of their knowledge of European legislation, good relationships with paint manufacturers and a feeling for what was important to painters, the vendors took an initiative. They themselves attended courses given by the manufacturer and then invited painters to come to the shops and attend workshops about working correctly and healthily with water-based paint. The workshops were a success. Because the painters had less work they had more time for workshops. And seeing as they were in the shop anyway, they took a few tins of paint away with them. This increased turnover and invested in customer contacts. Because the vendors likewise had more time on their hands, they went and gave workshops in vocational training courses for painters as well. That is how they acquired future customers. The paint wholesaler strengthened its market position through these actions. The company invested in the renewal of products, intensified the customer contact, broadened its product range, and paid attention to the innovation of products and services.

A third step was to be decisive and cost-conscious when taking action. When a director decided to leave, he was not replaced, and the director-shareholder took over his duties. He thereby demonstrated how he could also be expected to contribute to cost-conscious actions. The range was examined with a critical eye and stock management tightened, which freed up liquid assets. In the years that followed, the company took over six rivals who were not faring well financially. That is how the company created stronger market penetration and increased its scale, so that the running costs decreased on average. Purchasing paint in greater volumes meant that the paint wholesaler could demand better purchase prices from the manufacturers, which in turn raised the margins and further strengthened their financial position.

The paint wholesaler is currently faring very well, definitely in comparison with the competition. Its market share is gaining and its turnover is rising in a market which has contracted by 20 percent.

The lesson from this story is that the principal concern in times of crisis is not cutting costs and staff. Leaders who have a feel for the market, customers and the surroundings are able to pursue a new course in good time. If you as an entrepreneur see a crisis situation coming, you can invest in renewal and work in a market-oriented manner. A single-sided focus on cost cutting generates a negative spiral. It is precisely in times of crisis that innovative strength and customer proximity are the focus.

# Looking for places to cross

Once we are on our way through the unknown landscape, we keep on having to seek and find solutions so we can continue and complete our journey. Sometimes this creates tension in the group. We discuss these pressures with each other and always find a solution everyone can agree with. That allows us to go further on our journey.

21

# Management: the meat in the sandwich

*Managers as a special force in change*

I carried out the change project by the book. It was a merger of two companies in business services, and I had been
asked to supervise the merger process. I set to work enthu-
siastically. First the backgrounds and starting principles for
the new organisation were presented to all the staff. The
merger would result in a strong new company with more
possibilities in the international market. Nobody had to
worry about losing their job, and there would be many new
opportunities for further development of employees.

I gave all the employees a questionnaire so I could get
a picture of what was at issue. Business processes were
analysed and cultural differences were identified and
listed. The information from the questionnaires was then
discussed in group meetings with employees and managers. Gradually the contours of the new organisation, of the
work processes and the new company culture began to
take shape, with the strong elements from the two company cultures being retained. The strategic course for the
combined enterprise was determined with top management. Thus a picture of the current situation and the
future desired situation arose, and a change route could be
mapped out.

The new organisational form was presented to the
entire staff. Attention was also paid to the transition from
the existing organisation to the new organisation. Besides
the strategic course, the new work structure and the

desired culture, there was also attention for the integration process and the placement procedure for managers and employees. Nothing was left to chance and a lot of thought was given to the fair placement of personnel. There was a place for everybody in the new organisation. When the presentation ended, the people in the room applauded spontaneously. People recognised themselves in the story. The merger and the change process were accepted and they even generated enthusiasm among the staff.

**98**   On the Monday morning following the presentation I walked through the office and I felt it straight away: something was wrong. I just didn't know quite what. The atmosphere felt different. Suddenly I realised that all the managers' doors were shut. That was unusual. Normally all the doors were wide open, you met people in the corridor and had a talk here and there. Now an icy silence prevailed and that gave me an uncomfortable feeling. What was up? I had no idea, until I passed Steve's room. His door was open.

'So, hypocrite, cheat,' came the angry words from Steve's room.

I was taken aback. 'What do you mean?' I asked bewildered, since Steve and I had a good relationship and we appreciated each other.

'You messed things up and tricked us into it. You never told us the redesign of the work processes would mean that half the managers would lose their position of manager.'

'Yes, but... It was clear that the introduction of customer teams meant that the teams were much more capable of managing and organising themselves and that fewer managers would be required. And the basic principles of the new organisation included reducing the number of hierarchical levels. Nobody is going to be sacked or get worse conditions of employment; not the managers either,' I answered uncomfortably. But even while I spoke I felt that appealing to earlier principles was not the best way to deal with Steve's emotions.

My answer only made him angrier. 'You are not to be trusted,' he hissed at me.

We fixed things up between Steve and me, and also with the merger of the two companies. Steve taught me a lot. Superiors and managers are the builders and cultural carriers of the organisation. Getting them to participate in issues of content is insufficient if you don't pay specific attention to their personal experience, individual uncertainties, personal ambitions and motives. If these personal issues are ignored, you create a layer of managers who apparently do not want to change. The pressure from beneath is stepped up by participation of the staff who put new ideas forward. The pressure from above grows through top management's new strategic vision. You actually make a management sandwich: the pressure from above and from below squeezes management out automatically.

Input from managers is essential to the success of a change process. If that input remains limited to matters of content, we fail to appreciate managers as a special force in change. I learned from Steve that it is precisely managers who need to think together as well and to talk about their own role in the new organisation. Separate attention for this special group of committed people is essential to honest action and successful change.

## 22

# The power of conflict

*Why it is better to tell the truth*

The merger process proceeded successfully until it became evident that the commercial guys did not want to merge with the people from administration. That put the new work concept of customer teams in danger. I felt it would be wise to go and have a talk with the people from the commercial department.

In the conversation with twenty salesmen, the one salesman acted tougher than the other and they competed against each other on the sales they had achieved. You almost got the impression that the company could only continue to exist through their efforts and success. But it turned out that the largest turnover was achieved by people from administration who worked hard on contract renewals. The turnover from new contracts was less than ten percent.

In my talk with the commercial guys, I added: 'You shouldn't act as if you bring in all the money and so should have a higher status than the people from administration. Administration has much more contact with customers and ninety percent of all business comes from contract renewals which the administration staff take care of. The administration is more commercial than the lot of you put together, so there is no reason to be that arrogant.'

This statement brought the meeting to an explosive end. People walked away swearing and let me know in no uncertain terms that they wouldn't be talking to me ever again.

After this dramatic end, I went directly to Peter, the chairman of the board. 'I screwed up the project,' I announced straight away.

'Just sit down for a moment. Tell me: what happened?'

While I told my story, I saw a twinkle in his eyes which I didn't understand. 'Can you think of a way to tackle it further now?' he asked me. Together we sat down and developed various interventions to get the process running smoothly again.

Then he asked me: 'Which of these alternatives would you choose?'

When I had answered this question, he said calmly: 'Then I would just go and do that one if I were you.'


The alternative I chose was to collect more facts about the sales and turnover figures. I collected examples of successful and missed sales and contract renewals of the administrative staff and the sales staff. From sales files and customers I found out why a sale or renewal did not go ahead. I also searched for positive examples of sales and administrative staff achieving results through cooperation. Then I organised an afternoon and evening to which I invited salesmen, administrative staff and customers. That afternoon real customer experiences and the discussion about positive results created an agreeable atmosphere. The evening was for presenting the negative customer experiences. The customer stories showed that sales fell through because of delays and administrative ballast which came about through the combination of commerce and administration.

In a second session we examined the actual turnover and sales figures of commerce and administration. We looked for bottlenecks in real-life cases and thought about how they could be tackled. Gradually people began to appreciate each other's strengths and contributions to turnover and results. A third session was needed to forge cooperative working arrangements and work out new methods of working. Bringing commerce and adminis-tration together in customer-oriented teams was still a step too far, but the foundation had been laid. In the new organisational plan, business units were formed around customer groups. Space inside the new business units allowed each unit to set up the relationship between commerce and administration as it saw fit. Four of the five units chose for integral customer teams. The unit for service to large international companies kept its own commercial department.

In later discussions with commercial employees we enjoyed a good laugh about the session where I was left behind alone by cursing salesmen. 'Well, actually you were right, but of course we couldn't show that to each other. We were so keen on sales figures and competition among each other that it would have been a sign of weakness to acknowledge that you were right. We just couldn't do that. And you also denigrated us with your sharp tongue; we weren't going to sit down and accept that. We were also angry because it became clear that we weren't half as commercial as we should have been and we were concerned about ourselves more than anything. Perhaps we were angriest with ourselves, but of course that wasn't possible because we were the heroes of the organisation, at least, that's how we saw ourselves. You were a good distractor and outsider we could vent our aggression on.'
It was also instructive to look back with the chairman of the board. He had this to say about it: 'The situation in commerce made me much more aware of positive and negative signals and how I should weigh them up. Since I've been chairman of the board, people don't tell me any more what kinds of things they have done clumsily. I real-

ised that any information I received was always distorted and that I was involved less in the deliberations of people before they presented me with a decision. I thought it was wonderful the way you came in, to listen to your story and consider strategies together. Moreover, I felt you had done nothing wrong. Sometimes you have to tell the naked truth and let things escalate. Otherwise you will never get things moving. The approach you chose was really brilliant, especially by bringing the outside world in and getting customers to tell their stories. The salesmen can't object to that, of course. And discussing the positive and negative examples, using factual cases, had a very good effect. You connected with their emotions and ambitions. Perhaps you were too rough at first, but after that you took it up very cleverly.'

His conclusion surprised me. In my eyes, it was the chairman of the board himself who had helped me to make the right decisions, and I hadn't really thought those interventions through all that precisely either.

The last lesson from this story is hopeful: you don't always have to get it right straight away where interventions are concerned, because you can always build further on previous interventions, even if they were not effective.

## 23

# Traumas

*Making the non-discussable discussable*

The change process at the mortgage bank was a smooth affair and the integration of bank affairs and insurance products went like clockwork. Now it was time for the board and the management team to take the final decision about the further implementation of the integration.

The board and the management team had already postponed their decision a few times. Each time they wanted some new information or they just needed to wait for the results from the pilot teams: 'It looks good, but let's just run the pilot to its end until we are sure it is all right,' 'I would just like to see whether customer satisfaction will also continue to rise in the long term' and 'Has a risk analysis been made of the administrative organisation?'

Time after time there were new questions, without any decision being made.

Two months later the decision had still not been taken. 'We see that things are going very well and that the customers are satisfied, but...,' 'Yes, the people in the teams are working together fine now, that is great, but...' and 'I understand that the last technical problems have also been solved, but...' The part after the 'but' was not really important. No decision was being made. People in the organisation had started talking about it, and the credibility of the board was coming under pressure. That also brought the progress of the integration into danger. Something had to happen. But what?

Like Sherlock Holmes, I started investigating the situation. Something must have happened. Something I couldn't see directly. First I went to talk with a few people. 'No, we don't take any risks here, we certainly learned that.'

'What do you mean?' I asked curiously.

'That's extremely dangerous.'

'What do you mean?'

'Look, this is a banking business, lad.'

And that is as far as I got. So I decided to delve into history. I found an article in the archives with the headline: 'Mortgage bank on the brink.' The title of a second article was: 'Mortgage bank on verge of collapse.' Both articles were fifteen years old. Finally I found a headline: 'Mortgage bank saved. Home owners out of danger zone.' What had happened?

I deduced from the newspaper archives that the mortgage bank had almost gone bankrupt by taking excessive risks in their lending operations. Lovely growth figures had been presented, but nobody had paid attention to the risks. When businesses went bankrupt due to an economic crisis and home owners had trouble paying their mortgages, the mortgage bank also got into difficulties. I spoke with ex-employees and learned that the management team had worked day and night for three weeks to clean up the portfolio, cover risks and safeguard mortgages. Camp beds were set up in the office, and people worked right through the weekends too. The managers at that time succeeded in saving the mortgage bank. The reconstruction showed that most of today's board members and managers were involved in that bank rescue operation from fifteen years ago. At the time they must have agreed subconsciously: 'We will never take any kind of risk again, it is too dangerous.' And apparently the experience had been so traumatic that it was not possible to talk about it ever again either.

At yet another meeting with the board and management, again no decision was taken. I asked off-handedly: 'Goodness, I've noticed that we haven't been able to come to a decision six times now. That creates a significant risk, especially for the reputation of the board among the staff and the future of the company. Are you perhaps scared of risks?' A deep silence fell. I continued: 'What actually happened fifteen years ago?' Now the men started shifting uncomfortably on their chairs. 'The bank almost went bankrupt, didn't it?'

With tears in his eyes, one board member said: 'That was a terrible period. We don't want to talk about it. We managed then. That's enough.'

'Why don't you want to talk about it? Isn't it wonderful that you saved the bank then? Tell me what you did at the time to achieve that success.'

It was playing with fire, I sensed that. A few moments later four men were crying and ten others were unable to utter a word. The story came out falteringly. They had saved it thanks to team spirit. They were ashamed that they had let it get that far. They were happy that they had pulled through, but they were not proud of the fact.

'So you never actually celebrated the fact that you made it possible for home owners to keep their houses, and that the bank still exists?' I asked, amazed. Their eyes nearly popped out of their heads. 'Instead, you agreed with each other never to take risks again, and because of that you are now hindering renewal and risking the future of the bank.'

The meeting went on for a long time, although little was said. Two weeks later the board and the management team decided to continue with the renewal, after a supplementary investigation into risk control.

Sometimes a change can come to a standstill and it is difficult to see clearly why. Looking for possible historical reasons can help in that case. Sometimes you come across events in the past which everyone prefers to keep quiet about. It is difficult to bring that obstacle up for discussion, especially if the experience was traumatic and people have agreed subconsciously not to talk about it ever again. But it is necessary to bring that experience into the open again. You can do that by connecting the experience with the present and the future. It is playing with fire, because you don't know how people will react. But doing nothing is not an option either, so it's best to take the risk and start a dialogue about unconscious drivers and dynamics.

# 24
# Emotions

*The hidden power of emotions*

The business analysis of a production company gave rise to a structural change. This would make the company more flexible and allow it to respond better to the market and customers' wishes. The number of hierarchical levels was decreased and duties were merged. This would also have consequences for the composition of the board of management. Examining it purely from an organisational management perspective, you could reduce the number of board members from five to three. I discussed the situation with the board chairman who shared my viewpoint. The board chairman agreed to talk individually with all four managers and make clear that there was no place in the new organisation for the director of commercial affairs and the director of business operations.

After a week I asked him how the discussions had gone. The interviews with the two directors who would stay had gone well. The board chairman had made good agreements with the director of commercial affairs about winding down and transferring his work. The man was close to retirement age and a good arrangement had been agreed. He had not yet spoken with Eric, director of business operations. Obviously this was going to be the most difficult discussion. I intuitively felt that it would be wise to rehearse the discussion with the board chairman, and we practised the conversation a few times, alternating between the role of board chairman and director of business operations.

One evening a session was planned with the board about the new work organisation and management structure. The new work organisation was clear and could count on everyone's support. Once this was clear, Eric grabbed a pen and then drew a management structure which suited the work organisation. He ended up with four business units. He drew five directors at the top of that structure. I was surprised and looked at the board chairman, who all of a sudden looked the other way. What do you do in this kind of situation as advisor or project leader? Do you leave the responsibility where it belongs, or do you choose to be open and above board, fully aware that you are doing the dirty work the board chairman didn't want to stain his hands with?

I hesitated slightly but then simply went to the board and drew two other possible management structures which both ended up with a board of three persons. 'This is possible too,' I said. Eric gave me a furious look, then turned pale and looked for something to hold on to there at the window. This ended the discussion.

I came to the office one day later. The receptionist confided to me that I would do better not to show my face in the directors' corridor, as you could cut the tension there with a knife and Eric had roared that he would break my legs if I dared to face him. I realised that my first intuition had been correct, but that in the second instance it had failed me. I should have checked whether the board chairman had held that discussion with Eric and what it had resulted in. That was a considerable blunder of mine, which resulted in me giving Eric an unpleasant surprise. It also looked as if I had played a trick on him.

A good arrangement was made with Eric, and within three months he found a new job as director at another company. His anger, denial and dejection quickly made way for acceptance of the situation and new energy to work on his future. But things never came good between Eric and me.

Emotions can play out individually, but they can also occur in groups, as was the case with a family agricultural machinery business. It was a great company which was already eighty years old. People in the company still spoke respectfully about the founder, who was the grandfather of the current director. There was also a lot of respect for the father of the director; he was a father figure for many of the employees. The company enjoyed a strong family culture. People knew each other and helped each other, and there was a strong community spirit. Conflicts did not seem to exist, and everything ran like clockwork. But then the company was hit hard by the economic crisis and agricultural machinery sales tumbled. The director felt compelled to concentrate more firmly on turnover and result. Department heads were instructed to cut costs, not to renew temporary contracts, and to call people to account for their contribution to the result. Under the pressure of declining turnover, the atmosphere changed from a good-natured family company to a more business-like enterprise. That aroused a lot of repressed emotion: 'It's not as pleasant here as it used to be; You can see there is a new wind blowing; The atmosphere has become a lot harder; It is so impersonal since the new director was appointed; The trusted family feeling has gone.'

The director noticed these weak signals and one evening he invited all the department heads to a meeting. He showed a film about a construction company that refused to acknowledge the financial crisis and wanted to maintain the existing culture. It ended up being ruined, so that everyone lost their jobs. The film made a deep impression. After the film, the director told a very personal and emotional story. He was proud of the company and of the people who worked there, he was proud of his father and his grandfather, and he wanted the best for the company. He said that perhaps he had not always taken the right decisions, but he had always acted openly and with the best intentions for the company and the people who worked there. After this meeting, the department heads realised that together they could ensure that the company had a future. Many were emotional when they thanked the director for the honest meeting and his personal story. The director and his people had come to terms with each other, and together they put their shoulders to the wheel to give the company a future again.

These experiences contain a number of lessons. All kinds of emotions play a part in every fundamental change, individually and at a group level. Those emotions might not be so visible, but they are certainly there and you can sense them. It is essential to have a feel for the emotions of others and for your own emotions, so that you are able to change while retaining respect for yourself and the people around you. You have the choice of allowing yourself to be dragged along by the emotional undercurrent, or standing upright in it. With fundamental change, you need strength and guts to stand in it and seek the heat. Harry Truman knew it long ago: *'If you can't stand the heat, get out of the kitchen.'*

# Resting and recuperating

We take the time during our trip to have a rest day every so often. We use these rest days to look back on what we have done and discuss how things are going. It is helpful to pause and share experiences. Once we have reached our destination, or maybe another destination, we have a bigger rest. We exchange stories around the campfire and share the things we have experienced. By reflecting on our trip we learn from our experiences, and the desire to go travelling again grows within us.

# 25
# Smart

*Emotionally clever is better than smart*

If you are working yourself to the bone on a change project, it can be wise to take a break every so often and have a look at how the change process is going. There are all kinds of ways you can do this. If you see change as an organised trip with clear steps and interim results, you can measure the progress, preferably by being SMART. Systematic changes and projects engender goals which are Specific, Measurable, Achievable, Relevant and Time-bound. You control the project according to time, money, effort and result. If you deviate from the intended goals you can take more time, invest more money, work harder or cut away at the result. It's as simple as ABC. But what are you actually measuring? And more especially, what are you missing?

What you don't measure are people's emotions and ambitions. You do not get a picture of the undercurrent, the cultural dynamics, the invisible tensions and hidden interests and conflicts. Nor do you gain any insight into why delays occur and why objectives are not achieved. How can you adjust a process if you have no idea what is going on and why things turn against you? If you look at change as an adventurous journey, then it will involve shifting climates and undercurrents. You cannot measure them, but you can sense them.

The change had started well. Although there had been a little agitation and uncertainty, those feelings were revealed directly when the chairman of the board gave a presentation about the coming changes. Everyone had been given three questions before the meeting: What makes me enthusiastic? What do I have misgivings about? What do I have a question about? The answers were collected on the spot and ordered, and the board chairman answered the most frequently asked questions immediately. That gave confidence. The positive start was also

evident in the signals the members of the change team had picked up in the corridors. At every change team meeting, attention was paid first to 'eyes and ears'. Everyone in the team was asked which signals and emotions were visible and what sounds they had picked up. The team discussions recorded increasingly richer and more tangible results. Team members became more and more aware of weak signals and struck up conversations with people in the coffee corner and at the copier. During lunch they would go and sit with different people and ask them how the changes were going. Secretaries and receptionists proved to be fantastic sources of information. And it helped to drop in on the board and the works council every so often.

After an intensive two-day conference with the entire personnel, we suddenly heard negative sounds: 'We worked really hard on it, but it will come to nothing,' 'Oh, you'll never hear of it again,' 'They probably already have a plan ready up their sleeves,' 'It's all fake.' In the change team we couldn't understand it at all. The conference had gone extremely well, and it had supplied a lot of support for the change as well as a large number of ideas. Employees had been really enthusiastic. How could the mood switch so drastically within a week? All ears and eyes were opened wide and chats were held all over the place. That produced a surprising picture. During the conference, a report of the previous session had been ready for everyone on their chair at the start of the next session. We had worked synchronously on those reports during the sessions. During lunch or dinner a special team worked the report out in greater detail, made copies and distributed them. On the second morning, breakfast was accompanied by a beautiful report with illustrations and text. People had worked deep into the night on that one. What was the problem? Enthusiastic from the successful two-day conference, the change team wanted to create a really beautiful final report with outcomes and follow-up steps. We also wanted to present the content properly and include atmospheric descriptions, brief interviews and photographs. It had to look splendid, with a good layout in a lovely book printed in colour. Producing a book like that would take three weeks. However, due to the intensity with which information had been provided during the conference, people had become accustomed to receiving immediate reports; after a week without hearing anything, they were disappointed. Now that we knew where the emotions came from, it was simple for us to react. We had simply forgotten to tell people what we were doing and why it was taking longer. With that knowledge, we explained why the report would take a little longer and we accelerated the production process.

Apart from the weekly 'eyes and ears' round, as a change team we regularly took the time to pause and reflect on the change process and ourselves. We would hang large sheets of paper on the wall and everyone would write their observations on them. We discussed them sheet by sheet. The first series of observations concerned the change process. What was going well and what was not doing so well in the change process? What were possible barriers which we should take into consideration? Who supported the change process and who might not support it? Which substantive bottlenecks had arisen? The second series was about our own teamwork. How do we work as a team? Can everyone play their role properly? Can you realise your ambitions satisfactorily? What opportunities are available for improving our teamwork? What tips do you have for the project leader and for each other? The discussion helped enormously to keep a finger on the pulse, share observations and intuitions, and agree on actions.

Besides the weekly thermometer and the monthly barometer, we also organised an occasional climate session with the board to share our observations and hear their observations and feelings. That helped us and the board to coordinate our activities. And if that resulted in the need for more time or money, that happened automatically, without any problem or negotiation.

During a change process it is useful to pay attention to the passage of time, time spent, money and resources. But it is not SMART. What is really smart is paying attention to emotions and intuition, time and rhythm, progress and setback, team roles and teamwork, cooperation and obstruction. Only by paying attention to climate changes and undercurrents can you really respond to what is going on.

## 26
# With friends like that, who needs enemies?

*About heroes and bunglers*

I was full of energy and enthusiasm in the seven years I
worked for a consultancy firm. It was natural that I took on
a leading role, since many of the consultants in the firm
were young. But after seven years I found it increasingly
onerous to take care of the agency, and I started finding it
hard to stomach the assignments. I felt my own development was stagnating. Time for a change. So I decided to
bid the agency farewell and go down a new path.

I told Peter about my intention to leave the agency. We
had been in sticky predicaments together, he as a board
member and I as consultant. We had managed every time
to complete difficult changes with success. So we trusted
and appreciated each other more and more. We had actually become buddies. If we struggled with personal issues,
a telephone call was enough to organise a talk with each
other in the same week. We would tell each other about
our dilemmas over a meal. Peter had taken me into his
confidence more than once when he had faced difficult
decisions in his career.

Today it was my turn to discuss my career. We met in a
quiet restaurant in Amsterdam, and when the main course
came I told Peter I had decided to leave the company.

He looked at me thoughtfully. 'Why have you taken this
decision so suddenly?'

I told him it was not sudden for me. The assignments
were all beginning to look the same, and I wasn't learning

anything new any more when I worked. I felt like a well-trained monkey told to perform the same trick over and over again. There was no challenge any more for me, and the situation had been like that for a while. What's more, I was sick of agency management. The agency had a good reputation and was in a good financial position. I wanted to spread my wings. I also told him that I did not think it was correct to shift the strategic course of the agency just because I myself had had enough of customers, supervising mergers and redesigning business processes. The people at the agency were excellent at that themselves. It was just that I was fed up with it. I thought it would be best if I left the agency so the people could stand on their own two feet.

'How do you know that the people can stand on their own two feet? Tell me, what percentage of the assignments and turnover comes in through you?'

Unsuspectingly I answered: 'Well, I don't know exactly, perhaps around 70%.'

'So why do you think that the people can stand on their own feet better? How many people currently work at the agency?'

'Seventeen.'

'And they're all married or live together and have children?'

'Yes, except for two.'

'So we're talking about around sixty people who depend on the agency for their livelihood,' Peter put to me. There was not much I could say. 'And if you bring in 70% of the assignments, the other sixteen bring in 30%. That is 2% per person. And you think they can stand on their own two feet without any problems. Well, I don't think so.'

My appetite was gradually waning, but disappeared entirely when Peter kept on going.

'It's great to be the hero of the company, isn't it? I bet that feels really comfortable. There can't be many people who contradict you, since you have made them all dependent on you. Does that feel good, that power?' By now I couldn't even get a mouthful down. 'And this is where you want to step out. You are ready to simply pull the plug out of the bath. Do you know what will happen if you do that? The bath will run empty and you will endanger the future of sixty people. And do you understand what would happen to your own reputation if the agency collapsed because you just needed to get out? The fact that you cannot get out easily is your own fault, nobody else is involved. If you make people dependent on you, you are responsible for them.'

Peter presented me with a difficult lesson. My enthusiasm and zest for work had run away with me. I had created dependencies unconsciously, and now I was caught up in them. I decided during dessert that I would stay at the agency another year and make sure everyone became aware of their own strengths and self-confident enough to acquire assignments themselves. This worked, and after a year the consultants took over the management of the agency.

This history taught me something else: leadership is not being a hero and taking on a pioneering role. Real leadership contributes to strengthening the community so that it can give shape to its own future. The trick is to make yourself superfluous. Peter and I are still good friends and I wish everyone had a friend who dared tell them the truth.

## 27
# Well-worn paths to failure

*Eight ways to bungle a change*

You can find many lists of success factors for organisational change, and likewise numerous step-by-step plans for avoiding problems. Actually it is a bit strange that there are not that many lists of actors relevant to achieving success. And lists of factors for failure are close to non-existent. What are the best ways of bungling a change?

**Create urgency**

Creating urgency is a good way of wasting energy for change, especially if that urgency is not really present or is only felt by top management. The idea that you need a feeling of urgency is antiquated and based on the incorrect assumption that people will only get moving if they experience some urgency. Urgency indicates failing leadership, and nobody is eager to follow a failing leader. Too much urgency contributes to paralysis. Pressure from outside can lead to opposition. People are quite prepared to change, but they do not want to *be* changed.

**Call in external consultants to do the job**

Another good way of frustrating a change is to call in external consultants. This can suggest management incompetence and a failure to appreciate the strengths and qualities present in the organisation. External expertise can help if the problems concerned are clear and the people with expertise are able to contribute to solving them. In

that case you can contract the improvement out to external consultants who can implement a standard solution
with their standard models. But for fundamental change
you need the knowledge, experience and commitment of
the people in the organisation. You don't want the experience to walk out the door with the external consultant,
but to become anchored within the organisation. This is
essential for the continuity of the change.

## Use ready-made solutions

Selling a ready-made solution helps to kill creativity and
make people sit and wait. Scepticism grows quickly with
ready-made solutions: 'It's all been thought out ahead,
they can work it out themselves,' 'Look, here they come
again, time to duck until it's all blown over,' 'I bet they've
been to a management conference again,' 'What problem
was this a solution for again?' Involvement decreases with
ready-made solutions, except for the odd prophet who
believes that the solution is the ideal one and for people
who behave like well-oiled weather vanes because they
find every change a challenge. It is better to investigate
problems together and look for solutions together.

## Steer and control the change process

The misconception that you can manage a change is
widespread. Models with eight steps are particularly popular. An illusion is created that you can steer and control a
change process simply by following the steps and that you
will achieve success that way. This might apply to change
as an organised journey, but not to change as an adventurous trip. Planned and controlled change does not suit
these times full of uncertainty, complexity and turbulence.
It is much more about finding your direction in stages and
enjoying what you come across along the way.

### Call it cultural change

The best way to make a change fail is to call it a cultural change. The organisational culture is about the identity of the organisation. It involves deeply rooted values and basic assumptions. You can't change those things just like that. By saying you want to change the culture, you rob people of their identity and security. Many cultural change projects target behavioural change. The implicit message is that the behaviour of the past years has not been correct. That is an invitation for resistance to change. And with

simple programmes for behavioural change you will never even get to the basic assumptions. It is more effective to talk about how you can strengthen the customer value, and to tackle the discussion about the organisation's business idea and what you want to retain or change of that. If you conduct that discussion carefully, the organisational culture will change automatically.

### Invest in people who resist

One easy way of increasing resistance to change is to pay attention to people who resist. Resistance can arise from scepticism, uncertainty or protection of interests. If you pay attention to people who express their resistance negatively, you draw attention to their arguments and feelings. That makes them become even more demonstrative, and they influence other people. It is sensible to take resistance seriously, but blatantly paying attention to people who are resisting is not very handy, because this is quickly followed by more people who want attention or who are influenced by the big talk of people who are uncertain or who are protecting their own interests.

### Leave implementation to middle management

If you want to bog down the introduction of a profound change, it is a good idea to leave the implementation up to middle management and turn all your attention as leader to a new initiative. You give people the feeling that yet another change is on its way, and that results in people just sitting and waiting to see which way things will go. What's more, the change is obviously not that important, seeing as you are paying attention to other things anyway, so why should employees make an effort to make it succeed? Profound change only succeeds if you as leader are visible in the change and you support the change.

### Intervene where it sticks

If changes proceed with some difficulty, many people intervene at those points where things are troublesome or stuck. This is not always a good move. It is wiser first to take a look where there is still some space and where energy for change still exists. This may seem to be coun-terintuitive, but there is a logic to it. If there are arguments about the content, it is better not to try to get your way on that point. It is more sensible to have a talk about the mutual relationships or share your ambitions with each other and the ways you can boost them. If people have negative, stereotypical pictures of each other, you can try a bit of image breaking by contrasting images sharply against each other, but you can also see what connects people. If the intervention is well-thought-out, you seek the places where there is still space for renewal.

In brief, if you do not want to change but you want to make it look like change, there are enough options for making a complete mess of things. The trick with change is not to follow the beaten track, but to find new routes in a well-considered way.

28

# Awareness

*About three forms of awareness*

When you look back over the adventures in this book, what you notice is that successful change is based on three kinds of awareness: external awareness, social awareness and self-awareness. These levels of awareness contribute to successful change and to your own development as a change manager. You can only be aware if you take a break and have a look at yourself, if you have the time to pay attention to others, and if you have the space to observe what is happening in your surroundings. Once you have been on an adventure, it is worth looking back and asking yourself what you learned from the adventure, how your experiences can help you improve yourself, and what you can do to prepare properly for a new adventure.

Environmental awareness is essential to successful change. You can only act proactively if you know what is going on in the environment, the market and with your clients. Change is foresight. A picture of the future creates support and commitment, generates flexibility and motivates people to realise that future. It helps if the vision of the future ties in with the ambitions of people who are participating. This shared vision of the future provides direction for the change, and generates energy for realising that future. External awareness is not only about the environment of the organisation where you work, but also concerns your immediate working environment and what is happening there. Use your feelers and antennas to pick up weak signals. Your intuition will rarely deceive you, so take it seriously. It is best to keep your eyes and ears open so you can sense what is going on. When you consider the organisational context, the art is in connecting with it as well as examining it. Appreciate people's cultural values and personal values and take them seriously, but do not consider them to be self-evident either. Develop understanding for your own cultural values and likewise, don't take them as self-evident, but develop resilience.

Social awareness means you invest in others and are willing to be open to the experiences and points of view of the people around you. The skill is in postponing your own opinion for a moment and first searching for what makes the other person unique and valuable. The question 'What am I doing wrong that makes him so mad?' can help you here. Create a comprehensive picture of the people around you and delve deeply into their roots, their personal histories, underlying motives and their doubts and fears. Avoid personal barriers and make sure it is easy for people to approach you and call you to account. You can support people in who they are and what they can contribute, by providing honest and positive feedback and expressing your appreciation of their efforts and contributions they have made.

And finally there is self-awareness. As leader, change manager, project leader, professional and consultant, it is relevant for you to know yourself and your origins. You start by knowing and accepting your own biography. What were important places and events in your life, who were the important people who shaped you into the person you are now, what are your fears and what are you good at? It is good to reflect on your interests, what has really always occupied you and what you are curious about. What gives you energy and what gives you peace? What are your most wonderful moments that you enjoy thinking back on? To get to know yourself, it can help to leave your comfort zone and explore new places and cultures. You get to know yourself in different cultures and new experiences, and you discover the peculiarities of your own culture. You have options for exploring different perspectives and seeing new possibilities. Ask others for honest feedback. Excellent leaders and professionals distinguish themselves from mediocre leaders and professionals by asking their conversation partner after almost every instance of in-depth contact: what did I help you with and what would it better for me not to do next time? Three viewpoints are important for giving direction to your activities: Who am I and what do I want to be? What is my purpose in society and what purpose do I want to have? Who do I want to connect with and how do I communicate with others? These questions are simple. The answers are generally a fair bit more complicated.

Environmental awareness, social awareness and self-awareness come together in a moral compass. That compass provides direction for your life, for your meaning for others and for your being. As a leader in change you cannot manage without a moral compass. When you are working on changes and innovations, the moral compass helps you to find direction and create space. One example of a traditional moral compass is the Feng Shui philosophy. Feng Shui comes from ancient China and it already existed as a compass more than 3500 years before the magnetic compass was invented. It is based on astronomy and was used as a tool to position buildings and also used for journeys. You can use the compass to establish the north-south and east-west directions. The yin and yang symbols also represent the polarity. They are opposites, but both are necessary and they cannot exist

without each other. Values were attributed to the poles in
Chinese antiquity:

- North: wisdom and tolerance
- East: humanity and compassion
- South: dignity and courtesy
- West: justice and reconciliation

The centre has the values of seeking truth and connecting.

The values of Feng Shui are actually constant human
values which give direction to our actions and which help
us on adventurous journeys. Feng Shui teaches us how
you and the people around you can choose direction and
can influence well-being.

# Reflections

The previous chapters in this book contain lessons about organisational change which originate from daily practice. The nature of the next chapter is more conceptual. It gathers together lessons about organisational change in a methodological reflection.

# The lessons in perspective

Organisational change starts with obtaining information about the organisation, the environment and the problem definitions which are going around. You use your first orientation to enter into relations and gain an impression of the relationships. You follow this first picture with a deeper investigation of what exactly is going on. Gradually you build up an increasingly clear picture of the company strategy, the work organisation, the business processes and the technological systems, as well as the cultural undercurrent which says something about what gets people moving, how people work together and which tensions occur in that. Once you have a picture of the ambitions and problems, you can set out a direction for the change. The task is to imagine the future and use it to generate energy for change. When you know what is going on and where you want to go, the trick is to choose the change approach which is most appropriate to the situation. There is no 'best' method of change, and choosing a suitable change strategy is a delicate process. During the change you encounter all kinds of issues which speed up the process uncontrollably and other issues which can block the process. It is good to be alert to these. If you keep your eyes and ears open and can sense how a change is proceeding, you can select interventions to guide the change in the right direction. It can help if you take time for reflection so you can learn from the change and start a new change. This creates a continuous process of change initiatives organisations can use to qualify for the future.

The structure of this chapter follows the lessons from the previous chapters. The following topics are discussed in order:

1. Orientation and open-minded observation
2. Diagnosing and penetrating the area
3. Formulating ambition and imagining the future
4. Choosing a change strategy and travelling through the unknown
5. Changing and coping with the unexpected
6. Intervening and looking for places to cross
7. Taking the time to evaluate and learn

## 1 Orientation and open-minded observation

Change starts with standing still. This means that it is worthwhile first taking a good look around at what is going on, and only then setting out a change strategy that you have thought through carefully. Orientation is about exploring the current situation. Relevant questions in that case can be:

- What does the organisation stand for?
- What is its common benefit?
- What influences affect it?
- How strong is the strategic awareness?
- Which factors are decisive for the success of the organisation?
- What goes wrong with how it functions now?
- What does the organisation not manage to achieve?
- Who is playing what game?
- What does go well?
- What drags on?

The art in orientation is to postpone your judgements, not to start thinking too quickly in terms of solutions, and to examine events from more than one angle. During orientation you already start forming coalitions and creating a support base for change. Building up and maintaining informal contact with representatives and key figures from different parties in the organisation is a powerful instrument for identifying and mapping out the political system and assessing possible problems during the course of the change process. The end product of the orientation is usually an idea for the approach to the change process which comes next.

## 2 Diagnosing and penetrating the area

During the diagnosis, information is gathered about how the organisation functions and the possibilities for change. The usefulness and implementation of an extensive diagnosis depend on the pictures you acquire from the orientation. The content and methods of diagnosis also depend on the history of the company, the customer groups, the products and services provided by the organisation, the company strategy, the size and structure of the organisation, the way the business processes are given shape and the level of cooperation. The details of the diagnosis are partly inspired by the nature and size of the problem and the available time. During the diagnosis you develop activities which get the change process up and running, such as providing insight into bottlenecks and global discussions of possible solutions. Ideas and visions are exchanged during the diagnosis. They form a positive contribution to the change climate. A support base for change is already built up during the diagnosis. Discussion of the results of the diagnosis results in greater knowledge for the members of the organisation of how the organisation functions and the relationship between organisation and environment. When you discuss the information you often already proceed to the development and introduction of solutions. The diagnosis usually switches smoothly into the outlining of a picture of the future and the selection of a suitable change approach.

### 3  Formulating ambition and imagining the future

When ambitions are formulated and a future is imagined, this generates energy for change. The outline of a future situation depends on the outcomes of the diagnosis. When business processes are redesigned, a global organisational design is often established first. This design gives the parties involved sufficient room for manoeuvre within the framework provided so they can arrive at their own interpretation. A first step is then discussing general criteria with which the new organisation must comply. Bottlenecks, solutions, points of criticism and preconditions become clear during the diagnosis. This clarity enables management to decide on the definition of the new organisation. Management then reveals the direction for change to the organisation. The pioneering role of management in defining the objective is essential to the success of the change process, because management is primarily responsible for the coordination of organisation and environment and for the setup of the organisation. Changes in the culture require management to take up an exemplary role. Taking action actively allows ideas for change to be appreciated faster, and it also boosts the implementation of the actual change.

### 4  Choosing a change strategy and travelling through the unknown

There is no single best method of change. The strategy which is chosen depends on cultural and situational factors. Choosing a change strategy is perhaps the most difficult task in organisational change. Six strategies are worked out below:

## Systematic strategy

In a systematic strategy, the problem of the organisation is assumed to be known, and the emphasis is on designing a new organisation. Management initiates and controls the changes. Experts and advisors play a part in the problem analysis and the implementation of the changes. The change is a once-only project with a clear goal and end point. The change process is terminated once the new organisation has been introduced and a stable end situation reached. There is little leeway for any differences of opinion, and if they occur they are denied or pushed aside. The implementation focuses on making the new organisation acceptable and finding solutions for resistance which may occur during the implementation. The systematic strategy can be considered an expert approach. The approach is target-oriented with contributions from specialists and experts.

## Development strategy

The development strategy sees organisations as a source of knowledge and experience. That can be used during the change process. Changes are realised gradually and organisation members are involved in the entire change process. Experts provide support based on their experience with change processes. The decision-making process concentrates on reaching communal goals through communication and negotiation. The organisation's capacity for change is increased by involving organisation members in the problem analysis and stimulating them to give shape to the changes independently. The development strategy is meaningful in situations in which the issue is not yet clear and the course of the change not entirely evident. The development strategy can be used as a participatory strategy with contributions from employees.

*Power strategy*

In a power strategy, top management defines the objectives and controls the change. Giving the order for a reorganisation is one example of a power strategy. Improved results and cost cutting are often involved. Middle management is ordered to realise the change. The power strategy assumes that people focus on their own self-interest. The desired behaviour must be forced through the exercise of power and threat of sanctions. The exercise of power often calls up counter forces, and this can result in problems with the introduction. The power strategy is only useful if the top manager really has power over people in the organisation and if the objectives are tangible *and* can be controlled. A power strategy can result in the short term in a change of structure and of management positions. Cultural changes cannot be forced, and nor can work processes be changed swiftly through a power strategy. Power strategy leads to only meagre long-term results.

*Negotiation strategy*

In the negotiation strategy, parties look for results which are satisfactory to all parties concerned. Often this involves negotiations between parties with solid and almost equally strong starting positions which are able to block change. The strategy assumes that people weigh up the costs and benefits and agree to a change if it is advantageous to them. Facts and examples are used in the negotiation process to convince others of the usefulness and necessity of the change. Every change process has moments when negotiations take place, for example between the board and the works council, or between two merger partners who each try to clarify their position to the other.

*Learning strategy*

The underlying concept of the learning strategy is that people act on the basis of assumptions, emotions, feel-

ings and subconscious patterns. When people become
aware of these assumptions and patterns, space is created
for learning processes in which people can change their
behaviour. The learning strategy concentrates on discovering emotions and patterns that have an obstructive
effect. The idea is that learning comes about in a cyclic
process in which concrete experiences are followed by
reflective observations of these experiences. These reflections are then analysed and processed into new concepts
and interpretations of reality. By recognising and deal-
ing with restrictive beliefs, we can create new pictures of
reality. Learning processes almost always receive attention
in cultural change. The learning strategy is rarely used on
its own and is almost always combined with other change
strategies, whereby the development strategy and the
dialogue strategy are the most obvious.

*Dialogue strategy*
Change comes about in the dialogue strategy through the
exchange of ideas about organising, changing and inno-
vating. The aim is to find out the issues and look for new
possibilities. The strategy assumes that people are prepared
to take responsibility and want to accomplish something. The idea is also that people want to work together
and want to develop themselves as well. By entering into
dialogue with each other, people attempt to make complex
issues understandable and clear. Together they seek new
possibilities for giving shape to the future. In most cases
this approach results in positive effects for customers.
There is a great capacity for change because people in the
organisation learn how to use their own strengths to give
shape to change. This approach can be chosen if people
from several organisations want to cooperate and make
something new. Despite the positive experiences with this
strategy, very few managers choose it to get change going.

### 5 Changing and coping with the unexpected

The actual change is characterised by further elaboration and introduction of the desired situation. Strategic renewal requires a subtle interplay between internal and external actors. The social meaning of the enterprise is involved, as well as the search for new paths for realising that meaning. New strategic concepts and ways of working develop gradually. Business strategy, business processes, work processes, department duties, relationships between departments, forms of consultation and necessary training are elaborated step by step. Innovation processes usually occur in fits and starts, with periods of acceleration and of slowing down. Space is provided for innovative experiments by people who manage to find each other. Cultural changes are a matter of perseverance and creating the possibility, time after time, for discussing the things that are going on, what is relevant and what is not relevant, and the best way of tackling unknown situations.

Every drastic change process creates tensions between people from different backgrounds, positions and experiences. Conflicts can arise at a certain moment about the direction to be taken. These conflicts are normal and can even contribute to creativity in the search for new possibilities. If the conflicts are not taken seriously, there is a good chance that they will result in a blockage. It is therefore essential to recognise and investigate tensions and conflicts in a process of organising, changing and renewing. Interventions are used during the change to guide the change in the right direction.

### 6 Intervening and looking for places to cross

Interventions are concrete activities which help increase the effectiveness of an organisation and which support changes. During change processes you can use interventions which target organisations as a whole, groups and even individuals specifically. Interventions are also used to make the change process run smoothly and prevent resistance. A huge number of interventions is available. The choice of the intervention depends on the nature of the issue, the size of the organisation and the organisational level. Interventions can take the whole organisation as a starting point, or can concentrate on departments, specific groups or individuals.

My book *Cultural Change and Leadership in Organizations* presents more than fifty interventions along with examples, theoretical backgrounds and practical assistance.

### 7  Taking the time to evaluate and learn

In evaluations you assess what progress has been made, which results have been reached and how those results were achieved. When you evaluate progress and results, you also want some insight into the situation preceding the change. A careful diagnosis is therefore desirable. The aim of the evaluation of the change process is to learn from the change. By listing experiences and discussing the learning experiences acquired, you obtain insight into the realisation of changes and the success factors which play a part in that. This contributes to the capacity for change of people in the organisation.

# Successful change

It is time to give a moment's thought to the success factors for change. You will recognise many of the previous lessons. It is essential to have a clear mission and a clear strategic course so you can offer prospects for the future to people in the organisation. Environmental changes and market requirements are indicated explicitly, creating an external perspective on change. People often recognise this external perspective, and it helps them not to seek the reason for change in their own failings. If the vision of the future is not yet clear, it is advisable to pay attention to strategy development specifically in the change process. But it is not enough to pay attention only to strategy. Organisations are complex systems, made up of relationships between strategy, structure, culture, technology and human behaviour. With fundamental change, the point is to get the organisation moving as a whole. Successful change means that attention is paid to the harder sides, such as the strategy, the structure and the technology, and to the softer sides, such as culture, managing and patterns of cooperation. The softer sides are the least tangible and the most obstinate as far as change is concerned.

A shared experience of the problem is helpful in any change. If there is a serious crisis, management's task is to make the gravity of the situation clear and give people the confidence that hard interventions will safeguard the continued existence of the organisation. If the organisation is not in a situation of crisis and there is sufficient time for change, it is possible to arrive at a communal experience of the problem. The willingness to change increases rapidly if people in the organisation experience problems and want to channel their energy into solving them.

Having an inspiring leader who supports the change process actively considerably helps the change to occur smoothly. Active support from the top is necessary to realise drastic changes. Decisions about structural, cultural and technological innovations can only be taken at that level. Moreover, top management fulfils an exemplary function in the development of new cultural values. If top management does not function properly as a team, you first need to work on team development at the board level. Middle management also plays an important part in change. Managers often see changes as a message that their leadership is not satisfactory. They view the change as a personal failure. It is therefore wise during the diagnosis to make it possible to discuss the problems with which the managers are struggling. Managers also play a meaningful role in communication about the changes. They are often the first to hear the questions from employees about how the change process is going. If the managers are to give a good response to these questions, they need to be well informed about the direction, approach and course of the changes. When the new organisation is being designed, active involvement from managers is essential. Management courses about change processes can provide support for this.

Clear ambitions for the change are necessary to provide direction to the change and mobilise energy. Formulating ambitions does not mean that the change process is already fixed. It is advisable to make the approach to the change explicit as well. Communication about the direction and the approach of the change is essential. There are many ways to give shape to this communication: presentations for the entire company, discussion meetings and existing forms of consultation. Written information can also help to clarify the goals for change. Clarity about the approach reduces uncertainty and contributes to realistic expectations about the progress of the proceedings. Communication stimulates the potential for change because people are encouraged to exchange ideas. If there is a lack of information about the change, this can result in uncertainty and distrust and accordingly counteract the willingness for change. There are many options for disseminating information, such as company presentations, company magazines, information in the company newsletter, specific bulletins and the provision of information to customers. Information can be exchanged at conferences and in workgroups, information meetings, video conferences and computer animations.

There is no single best method of change. The art is in consciously selecting the specific change approach each time which is appropriate to the issue and the situation. Making this choice clear can make the change process more relaxed because people have a better idea what is coming and what is expected of them. A design approach is preferable if the organisation is in a crisis and a winding-down process is required. A development approach is better if the organisation wants to boost flexibility and innovative capacity. It is evident that achieving fundamental renewal with a pure development approach can be difficult sometimes. You can solve this by using the design and development strategies alternately. As the process progresses, the emphasis is put increasingly on the development approach. The dialogue strategy is highly appropriate for ambiguous problems and unpredictable events. This strategy is also suitable if several organisations are going to cooperate in networks or alliances.

It is advisable during the change process to make a list of those barriers which obstruct the effective introduction of changes. Obstacles can be found in the existing strategy, structure, culture, technology and the political system. Barriers can also come from earlier change processes which were not successful, and thus caused a lack of confidence in the possibility of actual change. Making these experiences discussable strengthens the idea that the organisation wants to learn from mistakes that were made and wants to choose a different approach now. The current method of management is doubtless also mentioned as an obstacle to change. Quite a lot of courage is required from management to discuss these barriers openly and find out how obstacles can be removed. For successful change you need to take the interest groups in the organisation into consideration: their goals, their sources of power and their power relations. Latent power conflicts lead to rigidity in decision making. Power problems at the top of the organisation can also block changes. Change is difficult as long as existing conflicts are not resolved and the division of power remains unclear. In addition, power can be put to positive use to solve conflicts, enter into coalitions and increase the possibilities for cooperation. A position of power can also be used to transfer inspiring visions, so that you create enthusiasm and generate energy for change.

Active involvement of organisation members contributes to the successful progress of the change processes. To build up involvement you need to inspire and consult. Inspiring contributes to the creation of a future perspective. Consulting results in better solutions being found for problems. By being involved actively in the change process, organisation members gain experience with change processes. That makes it increasingly easy for them to give shape to change themselves, and to react flexibly to changing circumstances. All change processes involve learning. In-depth learning in organisations provides a platform for exchanging and forming new visions of organising. Dialogue sessions are the place for exchanging perspectives on problems. Search conferences are helpful for developing a common vision of the future and translating this vision into the method of organising. Design conferences can support the redesign process. The learning capacity of an organisation is increased if you encourage and appreciate openness, and stimulate different perspectives of future possibilities.

A phased change approach helps to enable discussion and coordination within the change process. It is advisable to build rest moments into the process – times when you can study the change process itself and adjust it. Training courses can make the process of introduction easier and stimulate reflection about the approach of changes. The course should provide practical support in the daily activities and match the needs of participants. In courses specifically for managers, participants can support each other in realising change and new management methods. With behavioural change, it is essential for employees and managers to improve their skills together. It is precisely this kind of joint activity which can help in the way people in the organisation cooperate and achieve results.

# The end of a journey

We have reached the end of our journey through a chang-ing landscape. I hope the trip and the reflections about it
contribute to the success of people who take the initiative,
set off and reach their destination, with the knowledge
that the journey may well be more wonderful than the final
destination. I wish you much success with your change
process and the adventures it contains.

# References and inspiration

The stories and lessons in this book come from my own practice and reflection on my role in change processes. During my career I have found inspiration in working with others and in all kinds of studies and books. Below is a selection of authors and colleagues who have inspired me. I am indebted to them for what they have contributed to my insights. Perhaps they can also be a source of inspiration for others.

### Orientation of the area

Antoine de Saint-Exupéry, *The Little Prince.* Egmont Books, 1991.

Lewis Carrol, *Alice in Wonderland.* Bantam Classics, 1984.

Maurice Merleau-Ponty, *Phenomenology of Perception.* Routhledge, 2013.

David Erlanson & Edward Harris, *Doing Naturalistic Inquiry.* Sage Publications, 1993.

David Cooperrider & Diana Whitney, *Appreciative Inquiry.* Berrett-Koehler, 2005.

Yvonna Lincoln & Egon Guba, *Naturalistic Inquiry.* Sage, 1985.

Anselm Strauss & Juliet Corbin, *Grounded Theory in Practice.* Sage, 1997.

Russell Bernard, *Research Methods in Anthropology.* AltaMira Press, 2011.

**Getting to the bottom of the area**

Paulo Coelho, *The Alchemist*. Harper One, 2014.

Louise van Swaaij & Jean Klare, *The Atlas of Experience*. Bloomsbury USA, 2000.

Gareth Morgan, *Images of Organization*. Sage, 2006.

Peter Senge, *The Fifth Discipline. The Art and Practice of the Learning Organization*. Doubleday, 2006.

Geert Hofstede, *Cultures and Organizations: Software of the Mind*. McGraw-Hill, 2010.

Kim Cameron & Robert Quinn, *Diagnosing and Changing Organizational Culture*. Jossey-Bass, 2011.

Michael Harrison, *Organizational Diagnoses and Assessment: Bridging Theory and Practice*, Sage, 1998.

Charles Handy, *Understanding Organizations*. Oxford University Press, 1993.

Noel Tichy, *Managing Strategic Change. Technical, political and cultural dynamics*. John Wiley, 1983.

**Imaging ambitions**

Nelson Mandela, *Long Walk to Freedom*. Bay Back Books, 1995.

Jean Giono, *The Man Who Planted Trees*. Random House, 2015.

Melvin Burgess, *Billy Elliot*. Chicken House, 2001.

Arie de Geus, *The Living Company*. Harvard Business Review Press, 2002.

Alexander Osterwalder & Yves Pigneur, *Business Model Generation. A Handbook for Visionaries, Game Changer and Challengers*. John Wiley & Sons, 2010.

Otto Scharmer & Katrin Kaufer, *Leading from the Emerging Future*. Berrett-Koehler, 2013.

Kees van der Heijden, *Scenarios. The Art of Strategic Conversation*. Wiley, 2005.

Marvin Weisbord, *Discovering Common Ground*. Berrett-Koehler, 1992.

Daniel Goleman, *Ecological Intelligence*. Broadway Books, 2009.

John Hoyle, *Leadership and Futuring: Making visions happen*. Corwin, 2006.

**Travelling through the unknown**

Robert Persig, *Zen and the Art of Motorcycle Maintenance*. HarperCollins, 2009.

Magnus, Mills, *Explorers of the New Century*. Mariner Books, 2006.

Eduardo Mendoza, *The City of Marvels*. Pocket Books, 1990.

William Irwin, *The Matrix and Philosophy*. Open Court, 2002.

Jaap Boonstra, *Cultural Change and Leadership in Organizations*. John Wiley, 2014.

Léon de Caluwé & Hans Vermaak. *Leading to Change: A Guide for Organizational Change Agents*. Sage, 2002.

Henry Mintzberg, Bruce Ahlstrand & Joseph Lampel, *Strategy Safari. The complete guide through the wilds of strategic management*. Pearson, 2008.

Jaap Boonstra, *Dynamics of Organizational Change and Learning*. John Wiley, 2004.

Michael Beer & Nitin Nohria, *Breaking the Code of Change*. Harvard Business School Press, 2000.

**Tackling the unexpected**

Haruki Murakami, *Kafka on the Shore*. Vintage, 2006.

J.R.R. Tolkien, *The Hobbit*. Houghton Mifflin, 2012.

Paul Theroux, *The Tao of Travel: Enlightenments from Lives on the Road*. Mariner Books, 2012.

Andrew George, *The Epic of Gilgamesh*. Penguin Classics, 2003.

Tom Peters, *Thriving on Chaos: Handbook for a Management Revolution*. Harper, 1988.

Walter Baets, *Complexity, Learning and Organizations*. Routledge, 2006.

Karl Weick & Kathleen Sutcliffe, *Managing the Unexpected. Sustained Performance in a Complex World.* Jossey-Bass, 2015.

Robert Quinn, *Building the Bridge As You Walk On It.* Jossey-Bass, 2004.

Edgar Schein, *Process Consultation Revisited.* Prentice Hall, 1998.

Ralph Stacey, *Strategic Management and Organizational Dynamics.* Pearsons, 2003.

**154    Looking for places to cross**

Mahatma Gandhi, *The story of my experiments with Truth.* Create Space, 2012.

J.R.R. Tolkien, *Lord of the Rings.* Del Rey, 2012.

Jon Krakauer, *Into the Wild.* Random House, 1996.

Ildefonso Falcones, *De kathedraal van de zee.* Sijthoff, 2007.

Jaap Boonstra & Léon de Caluwé, *Intervening and Changing. Looking for Meaning in Interactions.* John Wiley, 2007.

Robert Quinn, *Deep Change. Discovering the Leader Within.* Jossey-Bass, 1996.

Karl Weick, *Making Sense of the Organization.* Blackwell, 2001.

Tom Cummings & Christopher Worley, *Organization Development and Change.* Thompson, 2008.

Wendell French & Cecil Bell, *Organization Development.* Prentice Hall, 1998.

Edgar Schein, *Organizational Culture and Leadership. A dynamic view.* John Wiley, 2010.

**Resting and recuperating**

Manfred Kets de Vries, *Mindful Leadership. Journeys into the Interior.* Insead Business Press, 2014.

Ken Wilbur, *A Brief History of Everything.* Shambhala, 2001.

Joseph Campbell, *Reflections on the Art of Living.* Harper Perennial, 1995.

Daniel Coleman, *Emotional Intelligence: Why it can matter more than IQ.* Bantam Books, 2005.

Campbell Jones &René Ten Bos, *Philosophy and Organization.* Routledge, 2007.

Willem de Liefde, Lekgotla: *The Art of Leadership Through Dialogue.* Jacana Media, 2005.

Donald Schön, *The Reflective Practitioner.* Basic Books, 1984.

Etienne Wenger, *Communities of Practice. Learning, Meaning and Identity.* Cambridge University Press, 2000.

Peter Checkland & John Poulter, *Learning for Action.* John Wiley, 2007.

# About the author

Jaap Boonstra is a professor of Organisation Dynamics at ESADE Business School in Barcelona (Spain) and Organisational Change and Learning at the University of Amsterdam (The Netherlands). As a consultant he is involved in change processes in international business firms and organisational networks in the Netherlands, Germany, Spain and South Africa. In addition, he is a member of supervisory and non-executive boards in financial services, engineering and the service industry, and also in public institutes in health care and safety. In all these professional roles Jaap supports leaders and managers in organisations to successfully achieve the changes they envisage.

At ESADE Business School, Jaap is involved in executive education on strategic and cultural change in organisations, organisational and professional development and cross-cultural mergers and alliances. At the University of Amsterdam he is guiding PhD students in their journey to gain more knowledge and gives lectures for master and graduate students in strategic decision making, cross-cultural management and organisational change and learning. His research focuses on transformational leadership, success factors to organisational change and innovation, power dynamics in organisations, cross-cultural management and organisational change and development.

Jaap has published more than two hundred articles on technological and organisational innovation, management of organisational change, politics in organisations, strategic decision making and transformational change in production firms, the service sector and public administration. His international handbook *Dynamics of Organizational Change and Learning* was awarded with the best contribution to organisational science by the Dutch association of management consultants. His book *Organizational Change and Leadership in Organizations* was nominated for Management book of the year. The Dutch edition of this book *Change Management in 28 Lessons* was in the top one hundred management books in the Netherlands for more than a year.

www.ingramcontent.com/pod-product-compliance
Lightning Source LLC
Chambersburg PA
CBHW020155200326
41521CB00006B/384

*9 7 8 9 4 9 2 0 0 4 2 9 1*